Ignite

Ignite

Lighting the Leader Fire

To Nancy —
Who is...
Only this time
in service of
YOU! ♡ Lael

LAEL COUPER JEPSON

For my boys and my beloved.
You know why.

Contents

Movement

Perspective

1

"So, let us push on now, and remember ourselves back to the wild soul. Let us sing her flesh back onto her bones. Shed any false coats we have been given. Don the true coat of powerful instinct and knowing. Infiltrate the psychic lands that once belonged to us. Unfurl the bandages, ready the medicine."
—Clarissa Pinkola Estes—

A Spit-It-Out Love Letter

I was running the other day thinking about you—and me. Us, really. And how we women just keep waiting for...what? To be ready? To be invited to the party? To be seen as valuable? For space? For time? To know the right answer, see the right path? To feel more comfortable?

I love you with all my heart, woman, but this waiting thing we do? It's got to stop. This is an all-hands-on-deck moment in our history, and ours are all bound up—not by someone else, but by our own thoughts about who we are and what we're capable of doing.

You are an untapped resource, woman, but you've yet to fully open the spigot of you.

Imagine what would be possible for our world if you did—indeed, if all of us women did. We could create a veritable feminine tsunami of change, seemingly overnight. Just by being more fully ourselves and trusting that enough to activate the power within us.

To put to use all that we've been given as women. To save us from ourselves. To lead us toward a new dawn.

Actively imagining that world in my mind's eye is what I do every day. Let me take you there. But first, I'll start with where we are.

Imagine you and I are standing on a beach at night.

All along the shoreline and far back into the land, we see houses on fire, burning. Smoke hangs and sirens wail. Beams crash to the ground and flames lick the nighttime sky. There is random yelling, and blaming, pushing, and shouting, but no one seems to be working together or listening to each other.

The very young are wandering around lost, wondering why the adults aren't doing anything to stop this, and the very old shake their heads with sadness, wondering what has happened to the world they knew and where it will go from here, long after they have left it.

People can be seen in pockets, standing along the shoreline, gawking, stunned and overwhelmed at how these fires got so out of control, trying to recall how long they've been there or where they even began. No one moves, it seems. They are disoriented, heartbroken, and exhausted after fighting the fires for so many years — a lifetime of years.

I look at you next to me, and I see you are feeling much the same way I am. We are disturbed by this sight but also somehow not surprised because our land has been burning for years. This is where we live, and for many of us, it's all we've ever known.

These fires raging across our land are a reaction to patriarchy — the structures that were made by a few and don't serve the many, the unchecked privilege and entitlement that has powered-over and pushed ahead to fulfill its own needs at the cost of others, the rules and governance that favor white men above all others, the industrial economy built on consumption that has little regard for the health of the planet or the people living on it.

Looking at the land as it stands now, it is clear this fire will rage until there is nothing left, and we wonder — as we would at the end of any loved one's life: Is there a chance of recovery or is it time to support a graceful death?

Do we hope and fight or do we grieve and move beyond?

I gently touch your arm to draw your attention away from the fires, and together we turn to look out across the dark ocean, feeling the cool breeze on our skin as it comes off the water, a welcome relief after having been scorched by the fires on the land.

It's dark out there and feels vastly unknown. So much is there, but unseen, which is scary. And yet, there is an expansiveness to the ocean. We sense it as it reawakens our skin, offering us hope even as it feels daunting.

We breathe deeply, filling our lungs with fresh, cool air.

I look at you and you meet my gaze, knowing what I will say even before I utter a word.

We can wait no longer. It's time.

I reach for your hand, look in your eyes, and say this to you with all the love in my heart:

*I **believe** women are the ones that will save us from ourselves right now.*

*I **believe** the world that men have made isn't working and that we're getting diminishing returns on the same masculine values.*

*I **believe** men are as exhausted as women by "the way it is" but honestly don't know any other way to be, other than what we've all been taught.*

*I **believe** the blessing of our times is that the levels of exhaustion, righteous rage, and dis-ease among women will unearth and wake us up to our innate resources.*

*I **believe** women will be the ones to integrate and intersect the whole of who we are, rather than dividing us further into either/or.*

*I **believe** women are leaving toxic organizations and burning houses in droves because they will be the ones to help us craft new, more vital models for how we work and live.*

*I **believe** that "toxic masculinity" is not solely about men but exists in women as well—which means our collective healing begins with each of us.*

*I **believe** women of color have been leading us for years with little to no credit and that white women are only recently arriving at this party.*

*I **believe** that rebalancing our world and our planet must begin with an infusion of the feminine before it can be reintegrated with the masculine.*

*I **believe** we are hungry for the leadership women can provide, but it will require radical and revolutionary change to create that opportunity—beginning with women's relationship to leading.*

*I **believe** white men will be asked to increase their capacity for discomfort, mess, and ambiguity as a means to decenter themselves, and it will be hard and loud.*

*I **believe** white women will be asked to more fully embody all forms of the feminine—ferocity (anger), power (voice), and agency (source)—as a means to own what's ours and stop asking women of color to do our work.*

*I **believe** we have it in us to co-create this next phase of our evolution and that it's happening now, whether we're ready or not, but it's going to require incredible amounts of bravery, creativity, and compassion by us all.*

I pause to catch my breath and notice you're holding my hand more tightly now, as if those beliefs I shared have forged a bond of understanding between us that is unbreakable.

We talk about what might be possible for our world if women were to lead us into the future. We imagine what might be different as a result.

More just systems, inclusive cultures, and respect for differences.
Less disease, violence, and war.
More environmental stewardship, accountability, and community.
Less mindless consumption, waste, and abuse of self and others.
More integrity, prosperity, and joy.
Less lying, patronizing, and manipulation.
More social justice, safety for our children, and compassion for all.
Less toxic workplaces, corruption, and unchecked greed.
More vitality, innovative thinking, and hope for our future.

That is what this book is about, my friend: Activating ourselves as women leaders on this dark night so that together, we might lead our world into this new future.

As the mother to two amazing boys, here is where I'll pause and clarify one particular point embedded throughout these pages because I want to be crystal clear from the start.

I believe men — and the predominantly masculine values they have used to design, organize, govern, and grow our world as we know it — are an *exhausted* resource. Literally and figuratively.

You won't see me paint men as bad, ugly, or wrong in this book — that's not what this is about. But you will see me refer to our founding fathers as tired, depleted, and maybe even a bit sour and brittle, like any resource that's allowed to be consumed past its sell-by date.

Where we find ourselves isn't entirely their fault, and for the many, many men I know and love, I don't believe it's even conscious.

But the reality is this: Men have been the face of sanctioned leadership up until this point in our United States history — indeed, the entire civilization of the Western world, and we are where we are as a result. Right here.

Which is why I am so keen on calling forth the women, starting first by looking at how we participate in, default to, defend, and ultimately perpetuate — consciously or unconsciously — this exhausted and combustible state we find ourselves in.

That sour — and often toxic — masculine energy lives in us women, too, and it's time to do a bit of a cleanse there as well. In my experience, this is both a deeply personal reckoning as well as a profound healing.

The gift of women — which has been both a blessing and a curse at times — is that we were handed the keys to the feminine at birth, whether we use them or not, whether we know what that means or not. It is presumed we know the way, which means we are granted more license to both access and express it.

Women possess the keys to the feminine because they house this ancient knowledge deep in their bones.

Perhaps it's because we cycle every 28 days like the moon. Maybe it's because we can bleed for days and not die.

Perhaps it's because women's bodies are designed to grow and support human life—even if we never have a child or have removed our uteruses—and so we know when we are in an environment that cannot support a human life and will either languish or leave—both of which are happening in epic proportions.

Maybe it's because women in ancient and indigenous cultures are known to be the gatekeepers of this sacred territory of our collective consciousness—the heart of the feminine, often referred to as the "wellspring," the "river beneath the river," "behind the veil," or the "Holy Grail."

Perhaps it's because women are born imbued with magic that allows us to intuitively understand what is not yet seen, said, or understood—giving us the ability to *feel our way* quite naturally through the dark or unknown.

I guess it doesn't really matter *why*. But the point I'm making here is this:

That key you were given at birth? We need you to use it, woman. And lead us there. It's time.

Until women find our way back to this place where the feminine lives and unlock it for ourselves, we will continue to reach for and deplete the very same resource that has been thoroughly exhausted — the masculine energy in us.

Which, if you're tracking my logic thus far, is a *direct* mirror of the state of our natural world and the environmental crisis we currently find ourselves in. Our house *is* on fire and it's raging hard on our earth.

Simply put: We desperately need help, and I'm looking at you, my friend. And us.

Imagine me standing on the beach with you now, telling you, "I know the way. And so do you... you've just forgotten."

You look back at me and say, "Um, okay, but how?"

I smile because I get that question a lot — in fact, I've lived it.

My story involved leaving that burning house to find the leader in me. I have spent the past fifteen years witnessing women figure out an answer to the very same question (*How?*) every day for themselves, and that is what we'll be diving into together on these pages. But know this: The answers you seek are right within you.

I know, it sounds like something Yoda would say. But more than an existential platitude or cliché magnet for your fridge, I mean it when I say this:

You are enough just as you are.

This is the power of the feminine to lead us forward to a new dawn — and women are firmly at the helm as we carry this GPS system deep inside us, and we can use it to help others plug into this wellspring in themselves.

This is why I feel so strongly about women leading us forward — not because I am one, but because we are quite literally born to do this. We've just either forgotten how, had that wisdom systematically trained out of us, or have believed what history has told us about women and our power.

We women have the power to change our world.

What our US history books have failed to teach us is that women have rarely need permission, authority, or even space to lead major political, economic, or social change in our world.

In fact, all they've ever needed is each other, which is why I'm gathering them here on the beach with us — oh, did I neglect to mention that it's not just the two of us here?

What if I told you that you aren't alone?

Sometimes that's literally the *only* thing that needs to be said to a woman to get her unstuck and moving.

I know this because I hear this concern from women every day — sometimes in back-to-back sessions over the phone or in my office in Portland, Maine. Outside of my work, I also hear it in grocery stores, coffee shops, school pick-ups, dinner parties, fundraisers, triathlons, conferences, elevators, and public beaches.

Am I the only one that sees this?
...feels this?
...wants this?
Why can't I just let it be?
What's my problem?
Am I crazy?
Is this normal?

Am I just delusional?
Is it just me?

So many of us women feel so very alone.

And what do we know about ourselves when we feel this way? We retreat. We mute ourselves. We pretend. We try not to feel what we're feeling. We numb ourselves. We betray the essence of what makes us women and checkout mentally, physically, and emotionally.

We call ourselves cruel and heartless things like crazy, stupid, loony, irrational, unrealistic, bitchy, control freak, insane, hormonal, chicken shit, or selfish.

I know this because I have been this woman. I know this because I work with these women, and I'm here to tell you that you'd probably *never* guess this shit is going on inside the heart and mind of a woman you admire.

But it is.

We hide it *that* well as women. That's how good we are.

Our bullshit narrative about women leaders feeling confident, fearless, and ready runs *that* deep and is, sadly, *that* misinformed.

The great and heartbreaking irony is that you'd probably see a woman you admire—maybe even me—and call her brave, fearless, confident, a badass, a powerhouse, or a force of nature.

This feels lovely and awesome in the moment to a woman, but to a certain extent doesn't really inspire her to do more of it because it actually triggers "imposter syndrome," making her think (silently):

Holy shit, if they only knew how I really felt... what really happened.

The fact is, that woman you admire *is* a badass *and* a force of nature—but not *all the time* and certainly not *all at once*. What you're seeing is the *result* of her actions, not the entirety of who she is or how she got there.

She is, in fact, like you.

But do you know that? Do you trust that?

I believe with all my heart that if enough women choose to trust themselves and what they have inside them at *this particular moment* in history, we will create a groundswell of change that is so desperately needed in this world.

We will create—collectively—a critical mass powered by women.

Here's what I do know for sure: It's not enough for any *one* of us to do this alone. We're beyond celebrating incremental changes and buoying each other and ourselves with "...we've come so far" and "change takes time...." platitudes. We can no longer feed the beast of doubt inside ourselves that tells us we're not ready or capable.

We have to change our narrative about how women lead.

The world has called us women to order, and we can no longer afford the privilege of feeling prepared or comfortable.

We have been called to figure this shit out as we go.

We need each other now. Which means we need you and your key. And that, my friend, is why I'm here.

Literally. I'm right here with you, having this conversation with myself, calling myself out, calling myself forward, to be of service and add my presence to this groundswell.

Envision this book as a different kind of fire. A controlled burn. A welcoming campfire at the beach that you can smell from a mile away — the one that lures you in from wherever you are, offering a bearing, an invitation, and a community in the dark of the night when you're too tired to sleep.

You may not see all of us but imagine women lining the beaches up and down the coastlines, our arms linked, some bursting out in song, others snorting with laughter or swearing like sailors.

Feel the powerful presence of women gathered in a circle around the fire that feels reverent and irreverent — as old as time and yet refreshingly new.

That's what I'm asking you to tap into: trust. In me, you, us.

Trust your senses to guide you here.

Together, we will keep it real and cut to the chase, blast through brittle veneers of doubt, revealing the essence of what we bring as women that the world so desperately needs.

We will illuminate the feminine face of leadership that is trying — begging, even — to come through us as women, to lead us all toward a new dawn, and get a clearer idea of how that looks in action.

Women's stories have the power to change the world. We know this, so we'll use these just as we always have: for inspiration. Only this time with a burning hot intention to connect those stories to women's leadership.

I will ignite this campfire for us using my own story as a leader, knowing that it's often easier to sit with someone else's story than it is to unearth your own. But then I'm also going to toss on our fire the stories of other women, too, because I know I'm not alone. And finally, I'm going to invite you to give voice to your own stories—maybe not with me but definitely with yourself.

One of my clients said it perfectly just the other day. She said she felt like the pilot light was on and ready but not being used. She was waiting. Maybe like you are now.

"It just feels like I need a flame within me to ignite," she said.

Let these stories—and your own— be your match.

Light your leader fire with this book, woman. Touch your match to it, and let nature take its course.

And if you find yourself resistant, doubtful, or too overwhelmed, consider that your head might be governing how you feel and check in with your body—because our bodies *never* lie.

And while your beautiful head is wrestling and weighing and deliberating, see if you can feel the beginnings of a red-hot ember glowing in your belly. That's desire.

The one that wants to come out and play with us at the beach.

And then ask your body this: Do you want to find out?

Do you want to know who you are without waiting? See what you're capable of doing?

All that ember needs from you is some oxygen—a simple puff of air to ignite it.

But it begins with calling bullshit on your waiting.

To be enough.
To be ready.
To know what you're doing.
To have a reason.
To be asked.
To have a plan.

At this gathering, you'll see all that cast off like unwanted clothes on the trail to the beach, so come as you are. Naked.

And right now.

The call for women to lead is *really* a call for women to create.

That's what quickened my pace on my run the other day when I was thinking about you, and me, and us, with Annie Lennox singing "Womankind" in my ear at deafening levels.

The change that's most needed in this world begins with women being who they are more fully and unapologetically without waiting a moment longer to activate themselves as leaders right now, figuring that shit out as they go.

Welcome to the fire, woman.

2

*"If you've ever really wanted to understand deeply
that to be a woman is to be magic, be in a circle of women."*
—Alice Walker—

A Circle of Questions

Long ago, when I first conceived of my business, SheChanges, I stumbled upon the book *A Circle of Stones* by Judith Durek. Something happened for me in that moment, and it wasn't until I read Diana Galbradon's book, *Outlander,* years later, that I got it.

A circle of stones is a powerful and ancient construct for women, intersecting the magic and mysteries we carry in our bodies with the earth and air of our material world.

Women come alive and remember themselves and each other in circles—we always have. The circle is home to us.

Which is good news for my own life because there is nothing linear about me and how I operate. I rarely read a book cover to cover, and the same holds true for how I write my books. I am constantly dashing over there and then circling back here, before adding a bit of something over there. And when I can't figure things out, I tend to spin or twirl — literally.

I've used this construct of a circle as an organizing principle of my business over the years — my blog is *A Circle of Stones,* and I host women's *circles*, not *groups*. The first experience I ever created for women leaders was called *Women of the Round Table* — as a nod to my love of the *Mists of Avalon*.

So, I guess it's no surprise that a circle is often how I hold my books as I write them, talking with my readers as if we have just stepped inside an ancient circle of stones far away from the center of town.

Envision this book as a circle with no true beginning and no real end. But if you look around as we gather at our campfire on the beach, see that this circle is contained by the presence of five very large stones, rather like Stonehenge.

I believe every good story is anchored by good questions — *What is that? Why is that? What if I tried this? Then what happened? What did you learn? Who are you? What lights you up? What breaks your heart? What do you notice? Now what?*

This love of questions explains why I have made my living by asking them — encouraging women to live into their own answers. But moreover, it reveals how I have found my way into storytelling.

Storytelling is one of the primary ways I lead.

Stories, as I hold them, are simply pieces of noticings that are woven together with curiosity and offered to the world — either visually or by the written or oral word.

Women do this all the time without realizing it, swapping stories at the bus stop, standing in line at the store, or sitting next to each other in a meeting or on the train.

Women are natural weavers, and their stories of lived experiences are what will bind us together in this time of great divide.

But do we see that power we have? And do we use it?

As I weave together experiences in my own life and my work with women over the years, I can't help but notice a clustering of questions that have emerged — my five stones:

Why me?
Why does it matter?
What's happening to me?
How do I do this?
How can I keep going?

Houston, we have a pattern — and an ancient one, at that. It seems women have found our way back to the center of a circle of questions, our very own Stonehenge.

When you consider how a woman grows, births, and nourishes another human life inside her body, these questions are often present for her. When you consider falling in love, these questions ring true.

Think about what you bring to a blank canvas, a vexing problem at work, an inconsolable newborn, a new business, a garden bed, a charitable event, an unexpected crisis, a once-in-a-lifetime opportunity, a campaign bid.

These questions call women to create. They galvanize us to action.

Something deep within each of us knows how to be guided by these questions — to see them as markers of movement — and yet...

we have forgotten them in our relentless quest for "knowing."

This is how a woman would lead if left to her own devices.

Inside these questions live our **desires** — the hopes, dreams, and possibilities that inspire us to get out of bed every morning and believe in ourselves and each other, to believe in the power of love, the beauty of our world, and the gift of contributing to our conversation. These questions ask us to unearth and give voice to what lives inside our hearts, so we might manifest it outwardly as an offering to our world.

Inside these questions lives our **humanity** — the very real fears, discomfort, and anxieties that bind us to each other as humans on this planet, reminding us that we are not alone and independent but connected and therefore interdependent. These questions ask us to reckon with our discomfort so that we can rein in our unchecked egos.

Inside these questions lives our **humility** — our insecurities, imperfections, and organic nature that remind us that we are animals and not machines, and as such are limited, inconsistent, and always changing. These questions ask us to live with the paradox of *I'm not that special/important* and *I am special/I matter.*

Inside these questions is **a call to action and service** — to assume responsibility for the life we have been given and to get busy living it as an active, creative, resourceful, and whole participant, not a numb, passive, or entitled spectator. These questions ask us to be self-serving so that we may be of service to others.

These are the questions of women leaders.

These are the questions of a seeker, a sojourner, a pilgrim. These are also the questions of a misfit, a rebel, an artist. This is me, and these are the people who gravitate to me. Maybe this is even you.

To be led by these questions requires a boatload of trust and a willingness to hold multiple truths. It also demands that we move in the face of the unknown, feel our way forward, and learn to navigate ambiguity, contradictions, and messy terrain.

Envision each of the five questions as a stone that will anchor our conversation here, and although I will be starting with one particular question, you are free to engage with the one that draws your attention most readily.

Beyond that framework, here's a bit of guidance on how best to dance with this book to help you to get your bearings:

O   Imagine this book as more a collection of essays woven together by a thread, rather than a linear narrative or chronology. Notice where you are called or pulled in this book and go there first. Start at the end, skim the table of contents, or the chapters themselves, and see what catches your eye. Meet yourself where you are, rather than where I am starting us. I offer this if you need permission to not read this in the typical manner we are taught — allow yourself to go rogue.

O   This is a deeply personal conversation with myself, yes, but it's also an invitation to engage yourself more deeply as a woman. So, when you see any reference to "her," "she," "me," "a woman," or "I" in any of the questions, quotes, or stories in this book, take that as your cue to turn those questions on yourself. Allow them to serve a dual purpose of revealing my story over here but also illuminating and informing your story over there.

O   I am choosing to have a very intentional conversation with women on these pages because that is my lived experience and is also the focus of my work. I trust you will opt in and out of this conversation as you see fit, regardless of your chosen gender or how you identify. This conversation isn't meant to happen to the exclusion of men or trans/queer individuals, nor is it to assume its relevance. It is, however, a very distinct conversation about the intersection of women and leadership, beginning with my own experience and liberally sprinkled with stories of other women I have worked with throughout the years.

O I've not invested a ton of time or intellectual curiosity on the more traditional constructs of leadership and leading, not because they don't have value, but more because there are riches to be mined beyond what we've been told, taught, and have collectively imagined possible. What I'm after in this book is the wellspring that lives *below* the surface of what we see, understand, and have already tried and tested.

O At the start of each section, I've done my best to paint a vivid picture of what that particular experience of leading change looks and feels like. Please resist the urge to see this as a formula, but instead consider it a "scratch 'n' sniff" invitation for you. Scent is a powerful guide for women, so if a description of a particular section smells good to you (*that's me!*), then go in there and see what's waiting for you. Likewise, if a description doesn't resonate (*I don't get it…*), skip over it or come back to it later. Trust your sniffer.

O If you would like to strengthen the muscles of curiosity and truth-telling with yourself or get a more targeted workout than just inferring meaning from the stories I've shared, I would suggest grabbing a fresh journal and sitting with some of the questions or **bold phrases** I've highlighted along the way. Knowing that this book at its heart is really a personal exploration with myself about who I am as a leader, these phrases are breadcrumbs that lead me back to the key insights

I've unearthed that I don't want to forget any time soon. If you want to deepen this conversation with yourself, look no further than what makes you uncomfortable or scared... then put the book down and take your curious mind there.

○ At the end of each chapter, I do my best to engage with you as I would a client who texts me on a Sunday night. As wonderful and validating as stories and examples can be, there comes a time when we just need a few specific breadcrumbs to inspire us to take action. So, I'll offer you what I offer my clients in those moments, distilling the essence of each chapter into three categories: *What I know for sure, Here's what helps, Resources for now or later,* plus one more (+) tacked on just for fun. This will be the grab-and-go buffet for those who want to get right to the heart of it and bust a move.

○ Let's disagree, shall we? I hope we do because we get to have different experiences and opinions, so to follow me blindly is to give me way too much power. Let's keep it real and tussle on these pages if you'd like — any part I play in sparking your interest or igniting a conversation with yourself will be my great honor. Let me be wrong and you be right. Or better yet, let there be multiple truths at play between us.

○ There is a *strong* current of beliefs and practices out there that will inevitably bump up against the pages in this book, so watch for the suck toward the mainstream current. This is not about either/or, but that might feel tested. You can have both, I assure you. You can bring your beautiful head along on this journey with you — we need it. AND watch for it to try and govern you because there is gold to be found below the head — in your body. So just notice what you notice, and do what you can to keep your conversation in your nether regions.

○ Don't wait to be "done" or "there" before you start playing with things, trying out some new behaviors, or sharing your insights with others. Be your own conclusion. Live your way into it—and feel free to come and go as you please. But don't mind me. Nothing would make me happier if at some point you put this book aside and went off and made a bold move of your own. That, my friend, is the point.

Let's get this party started, shall we?

She

Why Me?

IMAGINE waking up on a Sunday morning, feeling rested and relaxed. The sun pours through the windows and splashes on the bed, bathing you in sunlight. All is well and life is good.

You stretch luxuriously with your arms overhead, feeling like a cat with nowhere you need to be and nothing you need to be doing. And then, a sensation skitters across your consciousness, more quickly than you can track it, leaving you wondering if it was real or imagined. Except you know it was real because the sensation leaves a contrail like a jet plane across a blue sky.

Your mind is now fully awake, alert to a visitor that wasn't there just moments before — and you catch the scent of something foreign, beguiling, and exotic, and can't quite place it. But you want to.

Your brain immediately goes to work, beating the bushes and searching in the shadows for a clue that would help you identify this new presence that has found you.

Possibilities and questions start to flood your mind's eye as your busy brain holds up images saying, "Is this it? What about this? Oh, look at this one — THIS feels new..."

Your heart leaps into the conversation and gives a happy squeal of delight at what it's being shown — a seed of an idea, a glimmer of inspiration — and how it makes you feel. It feels like a party inside your body, with everyone jacked up on the possibility of something that has yet to be decided, acting like it's a foregone conclusion.

This is the sensation of being tapped — for something that is so perfectly and naturally you, it almost feels too good to be true.

You blush at the flattery of it because it feels like you've been singled out for being special — even as you realize that this visitor is simply inviting you to be more of who you already are in your heart of hearts, but in a bigger, bolder, and often more public arena.

And that's when your brain tries to shut everything down. Like a persnickety proctor catching you in the act of looking at someone else's paper, it chides you for attempting to cheat and reminds you to keep your eyes on your own paper. And then it tells you all the reasons why you're not really equipped for this challenge and aren't to move beyond the tasks on your own paper.

Except you already have moved beyond. Because while your brain has been busy prattling on and preaching about being practical, realistic, and reasonable, your heart has been having a pillow fight on the bed and is smiling at you covered with feathers.

Sure, it's messy and might take a bit to reorganize, but here's what I do know for sure: Once you get a whiff of those exotic spices and feel the feathers float down on your head, it's very difficult to be content with ketchup as your only condiment and an old backpack for a pillow.

That's the nature of desire getting activated—it rises to meet the new visitor.

3

*"If the first woman God ever made was strong enough
to turn the world upside down all alone,
these women together ought to be able to turn it back
and get it right side up again."*
— **Sojourner Truth**

Uncharted Waters

I had this dream years ago that still haunts me.

It's not a dream, exactly, because I remember being very much awake when having it. At its most basic level, it was a story I wrote one day, but it felt like something more in that moment—and still does now, years later.

Indeed, it is my belief that to craft a story is to craft a life and to understand this power is to forever blur the lines between making art and making reality.

To craft a story is to cast a spell.

The day I sat down to write my story wasn't remarkable in any way. I hadn't burned sage or set an intention. I wasn't feeling sacred or connected or even centered. I was feeling rushed and late for a call I would be hosting for six other women participating in my writing experience.

I grabbed my pen, turned to a fresh page in my notebook and began to write—just as I encourage other women to do when they are making too big a deal of it.

There once was a woman who....

My pen betrayed me in that moment, flying across the page, dragging the pinky of my left hand across the damp ink of the words I had just written.

My brain was left in the dust, freaking out and swearing at me that I was crazy, out of control, and totally off my rocker.

When the flurry of words ended five minutes later, I was out of breath and feeling like I had grabbed on to the fin of a big fish who had taken me for a ride and was just now letting me come up for air.

Random, I know, but bear with me here.

Because this story, while entirely made up, ended up being a placeholder for something I'd left undone.

I had yet to commit to being a leader.

Here's what I remember about the story I wrote:

A woman (presumably me...) walked down to a crowded wharf and purchased a ticket to go on one of the deep-sea-fishing charter boats for tourists. She was tall and had a determined look in her eyes, which ordinarily would have made her stand out, except that she was also completely naked. Her ticket was literally the only thing she was carrying—no bags, no jacket, no drink, no cell phone, not even sunglasses.

As she made her way through the crowds onto the full boat, people parted for her, staring openly at her nakedness, seemingly stunned but also sensing her substance and not wanting to interfere with the intensity of her mission.

She made eye contact with no one and trained her eyes only on the horizon as the boat moved out of the harbor. No one approached her, but her presence was palpable on deck.

Eventually, a new equilibrium was established on the boat, and people, being the adaptable creatures they are, adjusted to the nakedness of this woman and went about enjoying the ride, trusting, somehow, that the oddity of this situation would make sense eventually — or not.

When the boat arrived further out at sea and the fishing portion of the trip began, the naked woman became even more focused. One by one, she cast out a line and set up the deep-sea rods in their holsters until she had five rods in position and ready in front of her.

That's when the marlins started jumping, and all I remember at this point in the story is the small smile on the woman's lips like what she had hoped for was actually happening.

I remember writing that the marlins were like wild things fighting for their lives.

That's where my story — the one that felt like a dream — ended, and I was left with an inky hand, panting, like I'd just given birth to something.

With moments left before I needed to get on the call with these other women from my writing experience, I quickly Googled the significance of a marlin, hoping it would give me some clue to what the hell just happened to me.

Loads of references filled my screen for Hemingway's novel *The Old Man and the Sea*, and how the marlin symbolized something about Christ and communion and the symbolic ritual of the last supper.

Aside from that, I quickly learned that a marlin is a big-ass fish— like 16 feet and over 1,000 pounds kind of big.

I also learned that marlins are proud, stubborn, and tend to prefer their own company, confident they can do everything on their own.

So why am I starting this book talking about a big-ass fish and a naked woman?

Because that big-ass fish? That's the patriarchy. And I want us to reel it in.

It's important to note here, that up until the day I wrote this story, I never used the word "patriarchy." *Ever.*

I didn't think that word served our conversations about leadership moving forward, often making it synonymous with men, and therefore not a woman's problem to own as well. I'd witnessed too many women over the years point their fingers at men, many of them not taking into account how they might be culpable in having arrived where we are.

I've sat with this myself over the last fifteen years of working with women, and I realized I've been approaching my thoughts on the matter a bit…delicately…and diplomatically.

Or, as Rebecca Traister writes about her own experience of this in her book *Good and Mad: The Revolutionary Power of Women's Anger,* I had been tempering my truth with humor and sarcasm, which might get me a good laugh but can water down the potency of my soul-fire fury with a liberal dose of self-deprecation.

That's me, carefully masking my natural sledgehammer self.

Apparently, She's dangerous.

I hadn't been looking closely enough at the deepest desires and secrets of my heart. I hadn't gotten naked with my whole truth. I hadn't come out and openly shared the fucks that set my soul on fire, the ones I've been saving for magical shit. They weren't new to me, but I'd been keeping them inside for too long, and I wanted them out.

But feeling that fish tug on the line had the fire in my belly roar to life, and I started to see the patriarchy as a *system* that had outlived its purpose and was now destroying us by having us turn on each other.

And that naked woman?
That's what's being asked of us.

That degree of courage.
That degree of vulnerability.
That degree of focus.
That degree of audacity.

To do what has not yet been done. To rein in what has been running unchecked for too long.

On the pages of this book, you and I will be diving into what it means and feels like to be that naked woman on the boat, but before we do, let me just pause and point to one piece of that story you might have missed.

The way the crowds parted for Her.

Do you remember that? How they were stunned but also sensed her substance, respected her mission, allowed her to quickly alter the culture of the boat, even though they didn't ask her to or fully understand it?

We have that capacity within us to allow a woman to lead us, I know we do. We've just forgotten how. We've fallen out of practice, but like any other muscle, we can build it back up again.

It takes concentrated effort, dogged determination, and courage to offer the world an opportunity to practice following a woman's lead. That much is true, but it's happening.

It also takes a woman leader specifically articulating that she's a woman leader — and not just some random tourist on a boat.

Acknowledging you're a woman might feel like you're stating the obvious, but what you're essentially doing is saying this:

I want you to look at me. This is what a woman looks like leading. This is how it feels. This is what happens as a result.

Think of Serena Williams' loss at the US Open championship in 2018, and how she firmly took command of the angry crowds that felt she had lost unfairly and invited them to rise above the contention and follow her lead.

Think of Alexandria Ocasio-Cortez, a hardworking waitress from Queens, who felt so strongly about fighting for progressive action that she upset a 10-term incumbent and entered the main stage of American politics as the youngest woman ever to serve in the United States Congress.

Think of Ruth Bader Ginsberg standing firm and steady — almost always the only woman in a courtroom filled with men — as she deliberately and systematically unraveled complex legal arguments to dismantle laws that violated women's rights for over half a century.

Three very different styles. Three very different arenas.

The same big-ass marlin fighting for its life as women reel it in.

The woman knows. The marlin knows. The crowd knows.

They see it in her eyes — how she stands, rooted — that she's plugged into something greater than herself.

She's a woman on a mission.

When a woman taps into that degree of power in herself, gets naked with her truth, and plants herself firmly on our deck from her roots, she is unstoppable.

The crowds *do* part for her. The pointing, the jeering, and the mocking soon dissolve into stunned silence as *her* power acts as a stile to bring us into *our* collective power and frees us from the traps of our old stories that have kept us dead in the water.

We are more ready for Her than you might imagine. The question is: Are you?

There was a time not so long ago when I would have answered "no" to that question, myself, and it's because I was avoiding having a very pointed conversation with myself.

Let me give you the lowdown of where I'm headed with this.

There are two primary conversations I've dodged most of my life. The first I've referred to as "the woman thing," the second I've called "the leader thing."

The first conversation was the one I tackled in my book, *Unscripted: A Woman's Living Prayer*. This was where I dove into that first conversation with myself about what lives inside me as a woman.

My search and my stories led me to name and then define for myself the masculine and feminine energies that swirled and churned within me. I likened them to two unruly siblings in the backseat of my car, one I shamed (masculine) and one I silenced (feminine). In writing that first book, it was like we all pulled over to the side of the road and listened to one another, resolving to harness our collective energies to live with a bit more grace and power.

But that second conversation I've dodged... the leader thing? Well now, that's another story, one that I dove into here because I was simply tired of trying to outrun it.

Actually, that's a lie. I'm really good at running, and I had almost gotten away with it until a good friend busted me by pointing out how I'd artfully and consistently sidestepped one of the most obvious parts of myself.

My story as a leader.

I didn't realize I was doing this at the time, and maybe you don't realize you're doing it, either. But the embarrassing truth about me is it wasn't until I held the first version of the manuscript for this book in my lap that I realized:

Oh shit, I've done it again.

I'd written an entire book about women leading and had managed not to include myself in that conversation, choosing instead to hang out in the shadows of it where I could be comfortably out of the spotlight.

I was playing the hokey-pokey leader game.

No one was asking me to explain myself or prove that I was worthy. No one was questioning or challenging my beliefs about myself. No one was demanding a list of qualifications or achievements to ascertain whether or not I could, in fact, call myself a leader.

That was all on me.

How embarrassing. How exhausting. And how ironic, right?

That's when I knew I had — no, I *wanted* — to come out of the shadows and stand tall by this fire I have been kindling. That's when I saw how I had been dodging the very conversation with myself that I am asking other women to have with themselves.

I was affirming for others what I'd been denying for myself.

Let me explain.

My love language, so I'm told, is "affirmation." Apparently, this is my preferred mode of how I outwardly express my love — by telling people, frankly, the good things they possess that are patently obvious to everyone but that person, but often go unsaid. I tend to be the person who says those things.

Some people love by giving gifts, some by being of service, still others prefer touch to express their love. I affirm.

I have been known to stop strangers on the street to tell them they smell good. I have told a woman in the supermarket parking lot that her chiseled legs inspired me to lift weights more. I have told random people they have magic in their hands.

I have told many — strangers, friends and clients alike — that I am inspired by their courage, moved by their craft, in awe of their gifts, and gob-smacked by their determination, commitment, discipline, devotion, generosity, or chutzpah.

And it's all true. I affirm, but I don't bullshit.

Thankfully, my clients find this skill of mine to be immensely helpful and often hire me for just this reason.

You see, I work with brave women. As a brave woman myself, I think people often assume we don't need affirmations. They figure we *already know* we're fearless, badass, confident, and know what we're doing.

Which, of course, is complete and utter bullshit. Most of us can't appreciate how the hundreds of seemingly benign snapshots we offer up in our daily lives form a collage that paints such a clear picture for others.

So, I make it a point to affirm brave women. In fact, I make my living affirming these women.

You are worthy.
You're not alone.
You're not crazy.
You're onto something.
You are ready.
You are enough.
You aren't too much.
You've got this.
You have this in you.
You—and what you bring—matter.

I affirm women like you with my big and open heart, but I also bring the heat of my fire because when brave women start talking about their *bullshit* and their *asses*, affirmations alone don't cut it, and you know it, Sister.

I need to get off my ass and just do it.
I want to drive this shit like I stole it.
I need you to call bullshit on my excuses.
Feel free to kick me in the ass.
I need you to help me light a fire under my ass.
I need you to hold me accountable and ride my ass.
I need you to call me out and don't fall for my bullshit.

This is where the rubber meets the road for a leader.

My aim is to support myself and other women in defining what leadership looks like for each of us, gathering up *all* of who we are, so we can use it to be more fully of service.

Which means getting naked with our truth.

Knowing ourselves more wholly so we can be more holy—and of service.

My passion and my gifts revolve around debunking and distillation. You will experience both of those in here as I set out to poke holes in our myths, assumptions, and made-up stories about how women lead and move through change.

Imagine what you read on these pages to be the results of hours of conversations I've had — with myself and with other women — and that together, we will be teasing through the data, evidence, and insights I've collected over the years, tossing aside the traditional stuff we already know, have been taught, or already tried in favor of the new stuff no one talks about.

Imagine we are mining for gold together and are melting all those shimmering flakes down to reveal something that feels valuable, and perhaps ancient, but unspoken — distinctly ours.

Not *every* woman's, mind you, but ours.

Because women like you and me get that *all* boats will rise when one of our own rises. And we're all on this beach looking out at that open ocean with that look in our eyes of determination.

That's where we're headed. We're on a mission, and we know we're not alone now.

Women like us know how to raft up.

What I know for sure:

✓ Committing to being a leader will call you to reckon with gnarly things like your fear of being arrogant, not being enough (or too much), as well as the general corruption that is associated with that term these days. But do it anyway, because people don't follow a collaborator, strategic ally, or partner. They follow a *leader*. Rumble with this for yourself and you will be doing your part to heal it for us all.

✓ You can run, but you can't hide. Your essential essence will show wherever you go and will leak into every area of your life despite your best attempts to contain it, so turn around and face what's dogging you and introduce yourself to it. No one is as surprised by it as you.

✓ Getting naked with your truth means getting vulnerable. Expect vulnerability to make an appearance, rather than be surprised by it. There will be much more of this to come, so best to get on it now to start strengthening that muscle—you'll need it. As Brené Brown says, "You either do vulnerability, or vulnerability will do you."

What helps:

✓ In all seriousness, have a go at answering that infernal question that dogs so many of us: *Who do you think you are?* Only ask it this way, in the first person, so you're engaging yourself directly: *Who DO I think I am?* Not defending, pleading your case, or proving your merit, just state the facts of who you are and then add what's in your heart.

✓ What's *your* story as a leader? Do you know? Give it some thought. And along the way, desensitize yourself to that word by practicing it out loud and publicly. At work, say, *As the only woman leader at this table, I'd offer this perspective...* At home, say, *As the leader of this family, I'm going to make this decision...* Play with it other ways — *I'm going to take the lead here, I know myself as a leader, I'm generally the one people look to for leadership* — as a means to roll it around on your tongue.

✓ What would getting naked with your truth look like for you? Sometimes my clients practice blurting, so they are not rehearsing what they want to say or how best to say it. Sometimes they make a game of it like that movie *Liar, Liar* and pretend they are physically incapable of lying. Look for inspiration from people who do vulnerability well and see what they have in common.

Resources for now or later:

✓ *Fire Starter Sessions* by Danielle LaPorte.
✓ *Embrace Your Inner Girl* TED talk by Eve Ensler
✓ *ProtectHer* official documentary by Alexis Jones

+ *Erin Brockovich*, movie

"How we spend our days is, of course, how we spend our lives. What we do with this hour, and that one, is what we are doing."
—Annie Dillard—

The Waiting Game

If I had a dollar for every time I was told to be patient or wait, I would be a very rich woman, indeed.

The reality is, I suck at waiting, and people who tell me I need to be patient annoy me. There, I said it.

We have been taught that patience is a virtue, but I beg to differ. We're told that it's prudent to pause, wise to wait, and kind to concede or defer, and perhaps that is true. But when it comes to leading—especially *women* leading—those are the very beliefs holding us back. Those virtues have become the steel bits holding the wild mustangs in us hostage.

Here's an example. A woman hires me and sets context with this:

"I see myself eventually becoming CEO in the next three to five years, and I want to do what I can now to get ready", she says.

I look at this totally badass, highly educated powerhouse of a woman sitting across from me and ask her one simple and honest question:

What do you need that you don't already have?

She pauses, clearly taking stock and trying to grab ahold of something substantial that could be used to illustrate her block, developmental edge, or opportunity for growth — to prove beyond a reasonable doubt that she wasn't ready.

It wasn't a leading question — it was an honest inquiry — but you could tell her empty-handed response surprised her.

As it turns out, she was ready. There just happened to be a white guy in his sixties sitting in the spot, not going anywhere anytime soon.

This is not to say this woman didn't have stuff to learn or was done growing. We both knew that would always be a part of her nature; it's what she valued. But it is to illustrate this point I snag myself on constantly:

Wanting to "feel ready" is just "waiting" in disguise. Scratch that, it's actually fear.

Because from where I sit, I hear a whole different story when I hear her talk from her bones, not her head — fear lives in the head, truth lives in the bones.

If you listen really closely, you'll hear women talk about their bones a lot. In fact, one of my clients calls it her "bone-marrow truth," this sensation when what she's been carrying deep down inside her finally bubbles up from her soul and emerges into the light of the day.

"I know in my bones I'm ready. I just know it," she said.

When push comes to shove and all feels lost, women listen to their bones.

And that's what my client did that day after she had just gotten finished telling me all the ways she's stuck, messed up, and a lost cause — having rattled off everything from procrastination to perfectionism to overwhelm to waiting to paralysis to giving her power away to making excuses to being terrified to playing small to lazy.

I get it, I do. Part of me wanted to high-five her for naming all the shit that also dogs me. Part of me wanted to smile because she's not as original (or "broken" or "pathetic") as she might think — and I have an urge to call the woman who just sat in my office an hour earlier and conference her in, so I can prove she said the same *exact* thing.

But this woman is in her moment, and she gets to have it. Her bones are speaking, and when they first begin their grumblings from deep down in a soul, they often kick up all the shit and detritus that have been clogging the pipeline through which it was trying to express.

It's like angioplasty for the soul, that moment. And then?

She gave one big heave and up it all came. Her truth.

"That's all bullshit. I'm just playing small. I've been filled with tepidity and fear and felt stunted and hopeless, and I'm just not interested in doing that anymore. Whether I'm ready or not, my life feels like it's taking off, and it's just time to start living it and stop fearing it," she said.

And there it is. She sanctioned herself. Just like that, she validates her own damn ticket, puts her car in gear and starts driving. But this time she's going to do it her own way.

I want more of those moments for myself as a leader—those bullshit-calling self-sanctioning moments.

I want to be better about discerning that moment humility and the responsibility of preparation slip into politeness, being nice, and waiting my turn—or to be asked.

I want to be better about knowing where that line in the sand is for myself, so I'm not allowing the inconvenience or perceived disruption I'd cause get in the way of inserting and asserting myself as a leader.

But it's so damn sneaky, that hair-trigger response of not being ready. I'm guilty of falling into that trap, myself, and catch it years later when I watch my own tapes from my seasoned perspective.

When I was in college, in fact, and working at an overnight summer camp, I had my first experience of falling into that trap. I was offered an incredibly large responsibility—the safety of other people's children on a waterfront for a camp of 350 people—and my response, repeatedly, was "No, thank you."

"I'm not ready," I said.

He assured me I was and asked me to reconsider his invitation to be one of the waterfront directors for the following summer. It was quite an honor and we both knew it. It was one of the most coveted roles in the camp, and he had chosen me to be his successor.

This guy knew me well. He had been the waterfront director for many years and had watched as I learned to teach swimming that first summer, then go on to get my Water Safety Instruction certification so I could teach others how to be lifeguards, which perfectly positioned me to become an assistant director with just this moment in mind.

I was 20 years old and apparently ready, according to him.

He didn't suffer fools, this guy. And he knew what the job entailed with a ton of campers who were all required to participate in swimming lessons and open swim every day. It was one of those camps that centered around the lake—the water was where it was at—and here he was asking me to assume responsibility for all those lives in it, around it, and all that dark water that could swallow a body (someone's child, mind you) whole without anyone noticing.

I was terrified of his recommendation—promotion, really. I expressed this to him, along with all the reasons I was not qualified, capable, or mature enough.

Meanwhile, on the other side of camp, one of my best friends and partners in crime for waterfront and camp life was also being asked to be a waterfront director for the other side of camp.

His answer? "Sure!"

Mine? "No, not ready."

Now, I'm going to pause here and say something wildly unpopular—so much so it actually makes bile rise up in my own stomach.

Why is it a woman rarely considers she's ready for something until a man she trusts pulls her aside and insists she's enough or ready or a contender and should go for it because it's time?

(The feminist in me just cringed mightily writing that...)
And why is it that he typically has to ask her multiple times and

has to make a case for his opinion as if pleading it before the Supreme Court?

Yeah. I know, I don't like hearing that either. But think about it.

It has deep roots, that pattern, and I often wonder if we believe what we're saying in those moments, or if it's actually something we've been told women are supposed to say.

Maybe that's why I've been so drawn to the phrase "good enough" these days, reminding myself that most of my life has been spent actively figuring something out as I go versus learning about it in advance.

It's why I detest the question, "Where do you see yourself in three to five years?"

I don't want to know that shit now. Sure, I want some bearings to chart my course, maybe a really rough plan, but *knowing* for certain? Is that even possible? We're kidding ourselves with that.

Just ask the person recently diagnosed with cancer.
Talk to someone who lost her job.
Listen to the parents who have buried a child.
Talk with a couple that has experienced infertility.

You won't hear these people talk about their plans. You'll hear them talk about being present—savoring the moments as they happen. You'll hear them talk about the need to stay open to life unfolding and the resilience and resourcefulness of the human spirit to do hard things and figure shit out without knowing where they're going.

The ability to be with and move into the unknown.

If that isn't the essence of leading, I don't know what is.

Waiting creates congestion and constipation. Which is why waiting slows us down. It's hard to move while carrying all that weight.

We become full and bloated with ideas and inspirations, but we're so good at waiting and biding our time that we have either forgotten about them or are intimidated by the notion of inserting ourselves. This is our normal, and as a result, this place of waiting has become familiar, even comfortable.

Women are so damn good at waiting.

We wait to be heard.
We wait to be taken seriously.
We wait for our ideas to be recognized.
We wait for the opportunity to present itself.
We wait for our turn.
We wait to see if someone else will see what we're seeing.
We wait for permission.
We wait for respect.
We wait for validation.
We wait to have more seniority.
We wait to have the right experience.
We wait to earn enough credibility.
We wait to be ready.
We wait to be enough.
We wait for others to notice we're ready.
We wait for others to notice we're enough.
We wait for things to change.
We wait to be recognized as valuable.
We wait to be seen as equal.
We wait for the right time.
We wait for something to happen.

We just fucking wait. Why?

Because waiting has kept us safe at times — even kept us alive — so we could live another day to raise our kids, keep the job that put food on the table and a roof overhead, and make small but significant advances for ourselves like getting access to education, the vote, and our own bank loans.

We do it because we want to understand, listen, and be informed. We do it because we want to be respectful, considerate and collaborative. And yes, we do it because we want to be liked, be invited, and belong.

The ability for a woman to wait, it seems, has been a consistent part of her job description on this earth. After all, it takes nine months to grow a human being inside a woman's body, so we are literally born knowing this very skill.

We are taught patience is a virtue, but I'm actually wondering if this is the very thing holding us back from where we need to go to right this ship we're in and heal our world.

To say out loud that thing that will upset the apple cart.
To trust deeply in our instincts and make that game-changing move.
To go rogue and break rank from the "way it is."
To take a stand for charting a different course of action.
To have the courage to raise our hands and say "follow me."
To make that decision that will ruffle some feathers.
To stand out more boldly and be vulnerable by being the first or only.
To burn shit down, to rip it up, to say, "Enough—no more."

The process of waiting feels like circling the drain in the bathtub — around and around we go, caught up in something (or someone else's current) — leaving us ample time to reckon with our own thoughts, like the familiar doubt, worry, and fear that have us question if we're enough, ready, the only one, missing something, seeing clearly, or the right person.

No wonder so many women feel:
Alone
Scared
Crazy
Paralyzed
Frustrated
Overwhelmed
Sick and tired

Waiting keeps us circling Dallas, never actually landing the plane.

But here's the part we don't like to talk about as women: That steel bit lodged in our jaw that reminds us to wait patiently? More often than not, we women are the ones controlling the reins holding it in place, ensuring there is steady and firm pressure on that bit as a reminder to keep ourselves tame. And if one of us forgets and lets it slide out of place, we are quick to remind each other. We have each other's back that way.

I once worked with an executive who was a new mom returning from maternity leave. She had really enjoyed the pace and perspective that came from her time out of the office and wanted to see if she could parlay some of that into her work as she returned.

We spent some time exploring rituals and intentions for herself to support her transition back, and she played with some of them those first few weeks. At her next session, she reported back.

"Holy shit, I realized I don't WORK for the man. I AM the man…" she said.

When she pulled back from her own expectations, assumptions, and "rules" she had been carrying about herself and her work, she realized that most of what had been dogging her was well within her own control to change. The reins were in *her* hands.

Which, of course, then changed the focus of the conversation to be about permission, self-authorization, and the courage to stand out as different or (gasp) seemly self-serving.

But isn't *that* what is missing from leadership these days — the willingness for more leaders to be publicly vulnerable as they chart a different course and defy convention or "the way it is"?

This woman was brave as shit to own—and then use—her full power.

Another woman I worked with had left her senior-level position to go into business for herself. She had finally — and happily — extracted herself from this toxic organization where she had been run ragged, was always busy with endless meetings, and resentful (and full of guilt) that she didn't have much of a family life outside her work because she was so busy and distracted.

So here she was, free to chart her own course and call the shots. She came into my office one day shaking her head in disbelief.

"All of this time I thought it was the organization holding me back. Now that I'm out and have no one to blame but myself, I'm realizing it's me that is holding me back," she said.

Boom, Sister, Boom.

If waiting patiently is what we know how to do as women, it really gets at the crux of our conversations about how we lead, doesn't it?

Who would you be without your ability to wait?

Do you know? Do you want to? What if the world needs you to find out or, more to the point, *let* it out?

I've made a list to answer my own question.

I would be bolder—and more demanding.
I would be more resourceful and wildly creative.
I would be more experimental and curious.
I would figure shit out as I went and stop looking for permission.
I would have more fun with it, knowing I'm making shit up.
I would be more forgiving—of myself and others—as I go along.
I would be more inspired and less judgmental or jealous.
I would feel lighter and not so weighed down by doubt or fear.
I would use my time better—and be more efficient.
I would get clear on my vision and be less congested and foggy.
I would make a more aligned choice and cut the fluffy crap out.
I would be prouder and as a result more generous.
I would be more direct and not sugar-coat things as much.
I would ask for more and not see it as self-indulgent or greedy.
I would get better at receiving, knowing that I can't do it alone.

Consider this, Sister, and I will do the same:

Imagine inserting our thoughts into the conversation *before* we're ready. Interrupting a course of action *before* it's run its course. Or pouncing on a potentially defining moment *before* it passes us by.

What the world needs now is love, sweet love. Yes, that's true. But you know what else it needs? It needs women to be more impatient. More disruptive. More demanding.

Righteous Impatience = Deep Service

Spit the bit out. Don't wait until you feel ready or enough or right. Trust in yourself *that* deeply.

It's not going to be fun or easy as we storm this castle together, but just keep in mind that I'm with you, too, and feel the veritable army of women tackling this shit right alongside you, okay?

We need to practice the messy bits—publicly—to show people how it's done.

And by "messy bits," I mean making mistakes, being uncomfortable, demanding, commanding, vulnerable, visible, bolder, decisive, and yes, even selfish or bossy.

Oh, and let's do all this without necessarily being ready, confident, clear, or assured it will even matter or make a difference.

I know. Tall order, right? But there it is. No bullshit.

Here's how I'm learning to get through holy-shit moments, though. I shift my gaze to what's waiting for us on the other side of that big investment — like digging around for the prize in a box of Cracker Jack before you've even had the first bite.

And here's the prize as I see it — because here's what I know about women:

When you give her an inch, she'll treat it like a country mile because she knows how to be resourceful and get a lot of shit done with very little time and resources.

When you give a woman a dollar, she will not only use it to feed and provide for her family, but she will also invest in her community as well.

A woman, by her very nature, carries our universe in her womb — whether or not she's ever been a mother, carried a child, or still has a uterus. She carries that space inside her and as such is a living ripple effect.

Women are the root systems that connect us to the wellspring and the very planet we're on—our mother. They are born connectors who know how to create links in our chain and have the power to bind us (back) together.

All issues are her issues.
All children are her children.
All trees are her trees.
All injustices are her injustices.
All violence is her violence.
All heartbreaks are her heartbreaks.
All unrest is her unrest.

When women chose to move themselves, they will inevitably move us with them— which will be revolutionary.

So, fuck virtue. We've got that in spades. Let the wild rumpus begin, woman.

Let's rise now, not later.

What I know for sure:

✓ Excuses are seductive because they feel so rational. But they are really just fear cloaked in justifications designed to lure you back from the edge. And the edges are where the good shit can be found. If you value growth, learning, and change, then get really good at sniffing out and calling bullshit on your excuses. Because they will keep you smaller than you are and attempt to call it comfortable.

✓ *Yeah, butting* is the preferred sport in the cheap seats, not the arena, always game to lob back a reason why *not* to do something every time a *what-if* is sent your way. (*Yeah, but I don't have a trust fund. Yeah, but it's not so easy for me. Yeah, but I don't have as much time as you do.*) These are also the people who offer free advice about what you "should" do — it's easier to ask other people to hold our desires than it is to assume responsibility for them ourselves. But it is just that — a game — and nothing substantial or fulfilling generally comes out of it. Don't engage.

✓ There is a direct connection between the degree of shame we feel within ourselves and the degree of jealousy and judgment we experience toward others. Heal one, and the other will naturally dissipate. Notice where you are jealous, and it will point you to your longing that is being held captive by your waiting game.

What helps:

✓ Mine for gold using your curiosity. Ask with an open heart and all the sincerity you can muster, *What AM I waiting for?* And then listen to what comes up. Try not to judge it or fix it, just receive it as an offering of truth. And then? Resist the urge to explain why it's not true or dismiss it as silly or stupid. It's real and it's honest, so compassion is best here. Try this phrase on for size: *Of course....* It applies to practically every feeling or thought at these moments and gives it permission to exist, even as you move forward.

✓ Engage your fear directly because that's what we're really dealing with here. Ask yourself what scares you about taking action. And then when you hear a response, ask more questions to move you into that fear directly, to engage it: *What would I do if that were to happen? How would I handle that? What's wrong with _____? What if I did make an ass of myself? What if I am making a big mistake? What then?*

✓ Plug back into your *why*—the thing that's waiting for you on the other side of your reaching, your action, your effort. Rather than focusing on all the barriers, inconveniences, and distractions, see if you can shift your gaze to focus on why it matters to you. This will plug you back into your values. You have precious little time on this earth, so remind yourself where and how you want to invest it.

Resources for now or later:

✓ *The Call to Courage,* Brené Brown's Netflix special
✓ *This Time I Dance* by Tama Kieves
✓ Marie Forleo's *MarieTV* interview with Dr. Tererai Trent

+ *Working Girl,* movie

5

"I think the whole world has essentially been brought up not to be a girl...
I actually think that being a girl is so powerful
that we've had to train everyone not to be that."
—Eve Ensler—

The Feminine Face

For the past fifteen years, I have supported women in leaving organizations—high-performing, talented, educated, cracker-jack women who are paying out of their *own* pockets for my services—because they are done beating their heads against the glass ceiling, tired of playing the game, and smart enough to know there is more waiting for them somewhere else, even if they don't yet know where that "somewhere else" is, where it will lead them, or if it will be better than where they just left.

Over the years I've often wondered, "Do companies really *know* why women are leaving? Or do they *think* they know, but they really don't?" Even more to the point, I wondered if they cared to know.

I was recently asked to speak about this at an event called DisruptHR, and I decided to be frank.

I offered the audience a single "code word" that would alert them that a woman had already left an organization (energetically and emotionally), even though she might be there *physically* and still on the payroll.

An image of a white guy in his sixties flashed up on the screen behind me, and I said in all seriousness:

"This is Frank."

The crowd laughed, for sure, because that's what we do when we get uncomfortable in public places where truth is told, and it's frankly done with a lot of intention in the spaces I hold.

It's why I admire comedian Hannah Gadsby and her seamless weaving of story with activist spitfire in her Netflix special *Nanette*. She made the audience laugh, but she also introduced tension into that space with equal measure.

She was compassionate but equally firm.

"Laughter is not our medicine. Stories hold our cure. Laughter is just our honey that sweetens the bitter medicine," she said.

Brené Brown, a year later in her own Netflix special, would joke about that same nervous laughter, acknowledging that even if people didn't readily admit to it, she recognized the sound of "knowing laughter" because as a researcher, she hacked into people's lives for a living.

So, while the crowd laughed nervously that day I spoke, they were gracious and trusted me enough to receive stories about my work with women leaders that illustrated my point about our house being on fire.

I spoke about my experience of women who often—and unconsciously—use the word "frank" as a harbinger that they are, in fact, on the move and have either left or are making plans to leave shortly.

Can I be frank?
Let me be frank.
If I can just be frank…

My point was this: If a woman asks if she can be Frank, it's a rhetorical question. She *knows* she can't be Frank because Frank *never* has to ask permission to be himself.

When a woman asks, "Can I be frank?" she is letting you know she's about to say something that is considered socially unacceptable, organizationally off-limits, or a radical departure from the norm. She's about to stand out and reveal herself.

When a woman asks, "Can I be frank?" she's signaling that she's about to call bullshit on the way things are and is no longer agreeing to play along pretending things are fine. She's about to draw a line in the sand.

When a woman asks, "Can I be frank?" she is admitting she's tired of waiting and is done wasting her time (and other people's time) by talking in circles and playing games. She's about to pull back the curtain, cut to the chase, and point out that the emperor, in fact, has no clothes. She's about to make a decision.

When a woman asks, "Can I be frank?" she's poised to assert herself as the leader she is, whether it's in her own life or in the context of her work in the world. She's about to initiate a change.

From where I sit, amazing things happen when women give themselves permission to be frank because they are giving voice to what is bubbling up to the surface in us — our truth, our anger, our frustration, our ideas for change, our desire for progress, our hunger for movement — and have it be real, valid, and worthy of consideration.

In my conversations with women, we'll often take it a step further and consider what Frank would do...

He'd call bullshit on all this.
He'd lay it down in no uncertain terms.

He'd get in someone's face and call them out directly.
He'd speak up.
He'd say this is unacceptable.
He'd stand up.
He'd leave.
He wouldn't wait for permission.
He'd take charge.
He'd go rogue.
He'd get busy.
He'd talk to people he trusted.
He'd figure shit out fast.
He'd start making shit happen.

And there it is: permission, decisiveness, self-authorization, and commitment to make a move.

Thank you, Frank. Now step aside, please.

Because in case it's not patently obvious by now, Frank is the code word that the patriarchy is at work—which is something we all own, men and women alike— and it's also a signal that the feminine face of leadership is seeking to take center stage.

Please hear me when I say that I'm not suggesting a woman try to be like a man—that's not what this is about at all. What I am pointing to, however, is actually allowing ourselves to be *inspired* by what men have been granted freely in our society—the ability to set the agenda.

Women have a lot to say. It's about letting it out.

In many cases, green-lighting ourselves as women isn't so much about pushing down the accelerator as much as it is easing off the brake. It's about a woman giving herself permission to let the gravity of who she is carry her naturally forward.

Her presence, not her pretense.
Her authorization, not her title.
Her power, not her popularity.
Her instincts, not her positioning.

Having her lead with integrity, clarity, conviction, and service.

Like a badass boss of herself.

I once had a client who navigated this conversation with a fair amount of grace. At the time, she was a professional in her mid-fifties with her own business. She was incredibly successful, but she was also exhausted. Her body was tired, and her spirit was right behind it. And yet the demands of her business and her busy life kept asking her to keep pushing the pedal to the metal.

She sat down with a sigh on the carpet and said, "You know? I'm so tired of that idea of being self-centered..."

She went on to unpack that notion for herself, stripping away all the things our society attaches to it for women, things that keep us from getting our own needs met.

In a moment of clarity, she decided that she was simply going to reverse that idea, quite literally, calling it "centered on self."

Oprah Winfrey talked about this very thing so beautifully when she was interviewed by the Stanford Graduate School of Business in 2014. In reflecting on her life and her successes, she admitted that she used to be concerned about seeming too "full of herself."

You know what I'm talking about, right — that fear of seeming too self-important, arrogant, or self-serving? In our most sour moments, we might even fear seeming like a narcissist. Especially these days, where you can't walk two steps without crashing into one.

But at that stage in her life, Oprah chuckled as she reflected on how far she'd moved away from that fear, saying:

"I now see it as my job to be full of myself."

To understand, inhabit, and assume responsibility for the entirety of who we are, to be in full possession of ourselves so that we can do what we have been put here on this earth to do, each of us needs to be *full* of ourselves.

But it's hard if you feel like two people.

"I don't want to be two people anymore…I just want to be one," she said.

That was it. That was the moment this senior leader in her mid-thirties realized she had been fracturing herself in order to show up to her work as the person she thought others expected.

Like a wishbone, she had let the values and prevalent culture of her workplace gradually pull the flesh away from the bones of the woman she knew herself to be.

This woman, my client, realized that she had spent an inordinate amount of her time at work managing her thoughts, choosing her words carefully, censuring her comments, and not showing certain parts of herself to others, in an effort to convey a "personal brand" that demonstrated her ability to be commanding, in control, decisive, and strategic.

The way she described it felt like another full-time job, and it left her exhausted, frustrated, and resentful. She knew she was working way too hard for what she was getting paid, and to make matters worse, she felt distracted and inefficient, like she was trying to clomp around all day in someone else's shoes putting out fires.

This woman loves to work and has a lot to offer. All she wanted to do was to be able to do the work that she was born to do, naturally, without all the games, posturing, and positioning.

When we boiled it all down, she was tired and she was hungry. It wasn't the busyness or the challenges that taxed her as much as it was the lack of sustenance, which she knew she needed in order to function at that level.

She went about doing her work, continuing to get to rave reviews and promotions, and was frequently plucked out from her team to head special assignments, all the while being told how lucky she was and how grateful she should feel. She did her best to get the rest of her needs met when she wasn't working, which wasn't often, given the increasing demands of her position.

The tricky part about this strategy is that the better she did at work, the less time she had to access the fuel that helped her do so well at work. The more successful and valuable she became to others, the more depleted and resentful she felt.

Rather like the earth must feel these days as we keep pulling and pulling her natural resources from her without ever stopping to ask—or even notice—what she needs to sustain herself or stay whole.

Ever heard of a double bind? This is it.

She didn't allow herself to commune with nature for inspiration. She dismissed her desire to bring more color and natural light into her world. She tried not to think about how much she missed certain parts of herself—like being moved by meaningful connections, making things with wild abandon, or the serendipity and perspective that can come from travel.

Besides, that had nothing to do with her work, right? She'd have time for that later, she reasoned.

Except something was happening.

She was starting to call bullshit on the way it is.

Because gradually, as the wishbone in her grew brittle from tension, and more and more flesh got pulled from her bones, she started to realize that she no longer wanted to keep going like this. Something had to give, and she was tired of it being *her*.

This. This is the moment I adore as a coach because it's when a woman finally runs out of fucks, and she starts speaking her truth—however inconvenient that is to her circumstances at the time—and she starts to get really clear on what she desires.

This is the moment where everything changes and nothing changes, all at once.

She still was working, still had her position and her accolades and demands, but now she was armed with her truth and had plugged into her desire.

This is when she got out a red pen and started to craft a life on her own terms, in a way that felt good to her, and that was designed to help her stay whole so she could continue to be of service to others.

This is when a woman accesses her magic.

When she assumes the throne of her life and sees she doesn't have to sacrifice or twist herself into a pretzel to satisfy the demands or expectations of others.

She gets creative, resourceful, and demanding.

And just in case you heard yourself (or your head) say, "Well, that's not me…" or "I wouldn't say that I'm leader, really…" know that I hold the definition of *leader*, *leading*, and *leadership* as ways of *being* in the world, rather than a particular set of skills, an official position, or a résumé full of experience. You and I both know plenty of really shitty "leaders" that have all of those things.

What I'm talking about here is how you *use* yourself in the world — how you *choose* to show up, not about where you went to school or what you know.

It's about who you *are* and what you say yes to, not what you've learned, done, or know.

Years ago, when I first heard Elizabeth Gilbert's now-famous TED Talk on creativity, a spark of an idea was born in me.

Do you remember her talk? It was the one she gave right after she skyrocketed onto the scene because of the popularity of her book *Eat, Pray, Love*. She spoke about her experience of approaching creativity after success, sharing that many had wondered: How could she *possibly* ever write another word after having such a massive bestseller?

She talked about the concept of "genius" and how we had unfortunately strayed from the Greek origin, which held that genius was something that *visited* someone.

Understood in this context, a person then became a *host* to genius, but genius *itself* was its own fluid entity, free to travel about the populace, knocking on doors willy-nilly until one opened and genius was invited in.

It's about fully embodying what is moving through you at any one moment in time.

And then, apparently, we made a gross misstep that cost us dearly — somehow, we morphed our understanding of that concept of genius from being an energy that *visited* a person into one that *was* an actual person. As in: *That person's a freaking genius.*

Oh, dear. Talk about the haves and have-nots.

The original meaning was abundant, suggesting there was more than enough genius to go around, and that anyone and everyone could have equal opportunity to host it — all that was needed was to answer the door and say yes.

But the current meaning? It suggested it was rare, the privilege of only a few (hello, Frank) — not an arbitrary gift to just *anyone*, but to someone very special, indeed.

I wonder if we've made a similar misstep with our notions about being a leader?

After all, listen to how we talk about it today:

He's a *born* leader!
Not everybody's cut out to be a leader...
It's lonely at the top.
There are too many cooks in the kitchen.
She doesn't fit the leadership profile.

What if being a leader meant a particular energy was *visiting* us, instead of something we *were?*

What if we just made this all up, and something got lost in translation like it did with *genius*?

Wouldn't *that* upset our apple cart? But beyond that, wouldn't it also be less exhausting, more open and fluid, less arduous and exclusive? No tenure track and golden handcuffs. No more ivory towers, hallowed halls, and rarified air.

If you think about it, you might not even be able to *tell* someone had leader energy visiting them — it could be *any one* of us.

But I'm looking at women — specifically Wild Women.

Clarissa Pinkola Estes writes about this very thing in her book *Women Who Run with the Wolves* when she discusses the Wild Woman and how when women pick up her trail, she'll ride hard, break the rules, and stop the world:

"She is the female soul. Yet she is more; she is the source of the feminine. She is all that is of instinct, of the worlds both seen and unseen and hidden—she is the basis. We each receive from her a glowing cell which contains all the instincts and knowings needed for our lives."

What if leading were about receiving—and then passing along—a glowing cell?

Could it be that…simple?

Like Greta Thunberg from Sweden who spoke to the world's top leaders about climate change at the age of sixteen — and then went on to do a TED Talk that went viral. She acknowledged that as someone with Asperger Syndrome, she only speaks when absolutely necessary. "Now is one of those moments," she said.

Her point was this:

You are never too small to make a difference.

Think about Malala Yousafzai speaking out publicly at the age of fifteen on behalf of girls and their right to learn — something she knew would make her a target, and indeed almost cost her life when she was shot point-blank by the Taliban — and then went on to start a global foundation and win a Nobel Peace Prize.

Think about Emma Gonzalez, just an ordinary high school senior in Parkland, Florida, one day, and the next day, the face of an entire generation's outrage against the proliferation of school shootings as she stood behind a bank of microphones speaking about the need to ban automatic weapons, double-down on background checks, and create tougher gun control laws.

Think about Christine Blasey Ford, revealing her identity as the woman accusing Supreme Court Nominee Brett Kavanaugh, and then later publicly testifying to that fact after staying silent for over thirty years, and how her actions inspired more women to give voice to what had been silent for years.

Think about Anita Hill, who also spoke out nearly thirty years before that — only this time against Supreme Court Nominee Clarence Thomas — with the added risk of being a black woman publicly voicing her anger but before the #blacklivesmatter or #metoo movements could buoy her courage.

Think about Jacinda Ardern, the Prime Minister of New Zealand, the youngest female leader in the world (and one of the few world leaders to give birth while in office) and how she took firm and decisive actions to ban military-style semiautomatic weapons within *days* of a mass shooting.

These women are the feminine face of leadership, and yes, they are now public figures, but they weren't always. They were just everyday women living their lives until their leader fire was lit by something — a circumstance, an injustice, a crisis — and they were given a glowing cell and asked to take care of it for a while.

At which point they took a stand and spoke clearly into the bank of microphones.

The question is: Will you join them?

What I know for sure:

✓ Embodiment begins with the body, not the head. It sounds obvious, but it's easy to forget. Leadership, for women, begins somewhere *below* our heads — in our heart, our gut, or our wombs. And then it rises up through our solar plexus and tries to come out our throat, which is why it's useful to note when you bite your tongue or purse your lips because it's often a sign of keeping something in. Get curious about what's on the other side of it. Open up and say *ahhh*.

✓ The feminine face of leading is not about age, as many of my examples point out, but it is about presence and possession of self. It's in the very young, the very old, and everyone in between, so we're limiting ourselves by categorizing and measuring leadership potential by age.

✓ To decide to fully inhabit yourself — to fill yourself up with who you are — is to also agree to engage old and lingering fears like being selfish, greedy, or arrogant. Which means (you guessed it) more practice at being self-conscious, vulnerable, and potentially judged by another. Just be mindful of not participating in that shaming, choosing instead to see it as evidence of assuming responsibility for what you have been given.

What helps:

✓ How are you training people to be with you as a leader? By this I mean what cues are you giving them as to how to treat you, how to engage with you, and what you need in return? Do you qualify or preface your contributions in relation to another's? (*Someone might have already said this, but... Just to piggy-back on that thought… Did I miss something?)* Tune your ear to your own instructions, and maybe enlist an ally to help gather intel.

✓ Speaking of your body, when was the last time you were *in it*? I mean *really* in it, not just using it to move you from here to there, but dancing, laughing, sweating, breathing deeply, eating sitting down, making love with yourself or another, listening to music that moves you, stopping to smell the flowers or fresh cut grass, choosing clothes that make you come alive and feel sexy — as if you were your own special occasion, lighting candles with dinner, putting the top down on the car. Let her out to play and stretch her legs — and wings — and you will come closer to who you are.

✓ Make a playlist that is your soundtrack for leading. Put songs on it that make you rise and stand tall, some that make you sway or strut, others that take you to your heart and move you to tears. Spend time mapping the full range of your inner geography as a woman leader and give it musical accompaniment to remind you of what you might forget when the world gets loud and drones in your ear.

Resources for now or later:

✓ *The Invitation* by Oriah Mountain Dreamer (esp. 6th stanza…)
✓ *Mary Magdalene Revealed* by Meggan Watterson
✓ *Feminine Values in Business* TED Talk by Halla Tomasdottir

+ *Homecoming: A Film by Beyoncé*

Wellspring

Why Does It Matter?

YOU KNOW that sensation of being in a place that you've never been before, but... it feels familiar? It doesn't make sense, and yet... somehow it does?

That's how you know you're finding your way to the wellspring in you, that quiet, precious place where the crown jewels are kept. And you instinctively follow its trail, even though your brain continues to sound the alarm.

This is where we can start to hear the deepest part of ourselves — our humanity, even the planet. This is also the place some people avoid like the plague because what will we encounter there? What will we see and feel, and what will it ask of us?

You know you're approaching the wellspring when you feel the urge to go inward and put away your words. Time slows, the gears of your industrious mind grind to a halt, and there is this deep sense of listening that starts to happen — in the center of your body, not with your head.

Inexplicably, you are completely present and utterly moved by your surroundings. You become aware of your heart, beating all those years without being told what to do. Fluids in you start to thaw, then melt, and flow again. Tears well up in your eyes. Your breath catches in your chest. Gratitude washes over you like a warm shower in the height of summer, welcome and refreshing without being jarring.

Random memories start popping into your consciousness — and your senses are inundated with images and scents that plug you into what matters most — to you and to our world: love, beauty, vitality, connection, community.

Finding your way back to the wellspring within you — that source that is home to your spirit — is like drinking from deep groundwater after being parched and sun-blinded on the crusty terra firma, offering deep nourishment for your soul.

The wellspring is where the heart of the feminine lives, and once you find your way back to it, it's a game-changer. You remember how women were once the guardians of this source, and you'll get fiercer about being of service to it.

The trail back to it has long since overgrown from lack of upkeep, but here's what I do know for sure: It cannot be understood by our heads, only our hearts, and you'll feel the gravitational pull of it—like how the moon pulls the tides—the closer you get to the source.

6

"The world which men have made isn't working. Something needs to change. To change the world, we women need first to change ourselves—and then we need to change the stories we tell about who we are."
—Sharon Blackie—

The Other Way

When I was a little girl, I used to loll on my bed looking up at the ceiling when I was supposed to be getting ready for school. I used to wonder about things, looking up at that blank expanse of nothingness, untainted by nail holes, fingerprints, or scuff marks.

I wondered what it would be like if the whole house were upside-down.

I imagined what it would be like to walk on the ceilings and step up over a little bit of wall to cross over into another room and curl up around a skylight and be closer to the moon.

I thought of this the other day when a client of mine shared a picture of the most breathtakingly beautiful Christmas tree she'd seen on Instagram. She described an evergreen tree that had been tipped upside down, exposing its vast intact root ball, which made it look like the roots were growing up toward the ceiling. Instead of decorating the boughs of the evergreen, the roots were decorated with lights and bejeweled ornaments and tinsel, all in gold and silver and red.

She marveled at how something so beautiful could be hidden in plain sight, until someone thought to turn everything upside down.

That's the power of bringing some light and attention to what is often not seen because it's hidden below ground. It rounds out our perspectives, making us see the other half of the whole. It removes the blinders that have been keeping us and our vision for what's possible smaller than we are.

Think of a plant that stays a bit too long inside its pot at a greenhouse, one of the ones that don't get taken home and planted in someone's garden. Eventually, its root system overtakes the soil, which has no nutrients left, and the flowers fall away, the leaves start to yellow, and consumers pass it by, calling it worthless, unhealthy, and dying.

That plant never had a chance to bloom.

What if we are where we are because we're root-bound, having been stuck in the same pot for too long?

We have so many tried-and-true, time-tested ways of doing things. We have all these beliefs and ways of moving through life that we are so wedded to, we've mistakenly taken them as absolute gospel. In fact, we often refer to them as the "right way" or even "the way."

As in, "That's not the way it's done."

I beg to differ, actually. That's *one* way it's done. But there's also another way nobody talks about, or if they do, it's in hushed tones and confidences in darkened corners and hallways.

Let me give you an example.

A client I'm working with wants to quit her job that she's been in for years and years. She's good at her job, so there's no chance the company is going to let her go. She'll most likely be the last person to have her job eliminated, but there is this sense that there's something more out there for her. She feels pulled or called to something else…often wishing she didn't hear or feel it (*What an inconvenience, why can't I just be happy like everyone else?*) but secretly glad she does (*I just know there's something there, I'm starting to feel alive again, hopeful.*).

She wants to make her move and leave, and yet she doesn't know where she's going, what her next step is, or what it's even for. It's just this feeling she has.

So, she makes the bold move to invest in that feeling, and she hires me. We get to work. Things open up, get exciting, and that feeling she has starts to unfurl a bit. And then she eventually hits a wall. Right about the time she's taking herself and her desire seriously for the first time in a long time — perhaps ever.

"I want to move, but I can't see what's next", she says.

And there it is: The Way.
Making itself known.

The Way tells her how it's all going to go down, and it sounds something like this:

1. You need to have a clear idea of what you want *before* you take action.
2. There's only one right choice, so it's critical to be sure *this* is the one.
3. All decisions need to be made after doing exhaustive

research, thinking things through logically with a clear head, and giving careful consideration to all the variables.

4. You need to be comfortable, confident and secure before you begin.
5. You need to map out a detailed plan, pick the right and most efficient route from here to there, and create a schedule that you adhere to religiously.
6. Then, and only then, do you begin to act and put your plans in motion.
7. If you followed steps 1-5 properly, then everyone will support you and things will go smoothly because you've thought of everything, and it all makes sense and goes accordingly.
8. You arrive at your final destination just as you anticipated and exactly as you planned.
9. Everyone lives happily ever after.
10. People are inspired by you — your courage, your vision, your stoicism, and your ability to make it happen.

Notice the linear sequencing that suggests one item must be addressed before another can be looked at? Notice how pretty and neat and predictable everything seems to be? Notice how all emotions have been stripped out of that process? Notice how it all feels rather black-and-white? Notice how everything feels rather dire and full of impending doom — like if you fuck up, the space shuttle will crash land on Nantucket, or the entire communication grid will shut down.

Inspiring? Not much. Familiar? You betcha.

This is the model most of us have in our heads because this is the model written about in our history books and taught to many of us in our elementary schools and MBA programs.

And this model works. It does. It's *soothingly* predictable and definitely has merit, especially in times of war or a crisis. Think of a military operation, a financial acquisition, or a surgical procedure.

There's no room for seeing how it goes, feeling your way, or winging it in those instances. There's no time for coloring outside the lines, emotions, or shades of gray in those situations because it's all about the big P's: planning, preparation, protocol, and precision.

Thank you, military, and all those who serve in it.

But from where I sit, the only number that holds true for me and how I show up as a leader is #10 in that model.

So, this becomes the heart of the work I do with my clients — to hold space for a different (alternative, wild, even weird) model to move in and guide them.

This is the other way that's been living underground, in our roots.

Think of how a woman grows a baby in her belly and gives birth.
Think of how two people meet and fall in love.
Think of how an artist approaches a blank canvas.
Think of how a writer looks at a blinking cursor.
Think of how parents raise their kids.
Think of how an inventor creates something no one has ever seen before.
Think of how a toddler learns how to walk.
Think of how you learned to swim or ride a bike.
Think of how you experience orgasm.
Think of how a happy accident triggers an unexpected joy.
Think of how getting blindsided by something turned out to be the best thing.

Welcome to the other way, the one that cannot be contained by our minds and therefore asks our entire body to come to the show.

The one that flows up from our roots and doesn't trickle down from our heads.

The one that has curves, twists, and organic surges, instead of lines, links, and a mechanical engine. The one made of flesh and bones, not petroleum and steel.

The one that can't be measured, institutionalized, or replicated.

This way tends to be best understood in terms of a cyclical process, rather than linear steps, so imagine the list below being individual cabs on a big Ferris wheel—each one can stop, letting people on or off, but they are all connected to the whole wheel. It just keeps going around and around, so there's *really* no way of knowing which cab is the first or the last. It just doesn't matter.

o   There is an intense feeling—desire, anger, done-ness, hunger.
    excitement, jealousy, giddiness, heartbreak…
o   We get curious about the feeling, fleshing out that initial
    sensation, finding more words to represent it, and helping to
    give it shape and form, a name.
o   We track it back to its source, connecting it to something
    that matters—a value, a desire to be of service, have impact,
    address a problem—or create something that's missing.
o   We get into our bodies through movement, creativity or
    spiritual means—getting unstuck, outside the box, inspired,
    different perspective, fresh air.
o   We get quiet and listen deeply, notice what we notice, be
    with what finds us.
o   We get inspired, the fog lifts, possibilities start to emerge.
o   We set an intention by saying it aloud and having it
    witnessed.
o   We move closer to the feeling, create some structure,
    flirt with possibilities, send up trial balloons, play with
    experimental actions.

- o We pause and make note of where we are now, being honest—awareness, senses, learnings, shifts in perspective, what feels good, what doesn't, what worked, what didn't.
- o We acknowledge where we are now relative to where we want to be, tuning in to our feelings and senses to determine what we want more of or less of.

This is the way I've learned to move in my life. I know this way like the back of my hand, but I've spent most of my life only reaching for it when I was desperate and needing a quick fix, rather like the time I "cheated" in school by writing with my left hand when the teacher wasn't looking because I was told it was the wrong hand.

It's also the way I've called *weird, crazy, wild,* and *out there,* not because I believe it is, but because I was hiding my true beliefs from others who couldn't yet see this way.

In all fairness, it's hard to see the underground roots as beautiful when you're so conditioned to look at all those lush green boughs on the trees with pretty lights and colorful balls on them.

We've been trained to believe that only what we *see* is real and therefore valuable, but I know a different way.

The other way is native soil to women, which gives us added vision as leaders.

I hold space fiercely for women to experience this other way for themselves, and nothing gives me more joy than when they get a taste of it for the first time. People know this about me because I am open about it. Like my son, the day he insisted I watch a movie with him.

"It's got your stuff all over it, Mom. It's all about the work you do."

93

The movie was Marvel's latest called *Dr. Strange,* and at first blush, I was thinking it might be entertaining, but not all that relevant to me or my work within SheChanges.

Boy, was I wrong about the not-relevant thing.

This kid, it seems, knows me and what I do really well. More to the point, he'd managed to shine a light on *exactly* the vision I'm so keen on leading us toward and the role I feel women will play in helping us all to get there.

The premise of the movie is essentially about our ability (or inability) to believe in magic as a legitimate and powerful tool.

The main character, Dr. Strange, is a world-renowned neurosurgeon who gets in a terrible car wreck, leaving his precious hands — his instruments — destroyed. He tries everything to repair the damage to no avail, until he arrives, desperate, at the doorstep of the mystical arts.

A woman known only as The Ancient One answers his insistent knock and cracks through Dr. Strange's Western-trained rational mind to get at the world he was not allowing himself to see as real.

"You're a man looking through a keyhole, and you've spent your whole life trying to widen that keyhole—to see more, to know more—and now, upon hearing it can be widened in ways you can't imagine, you reject the possibility."

She invites him to stand with her at the intersection of rational science and the mystic arts.

This is where we're headed, and women are well suited to lead us there, not because it's fun or interesting, but because it's real.

The unfortunate trap we've fallen into as a result of much of our developed world being shaped by white, male Western values, is that we have embedded an inherent mistrust in anything we can't understand with our minds or measure with our instruments (including our need to see it with our own eyes).

Opening to magic and the mysteries doesn't need to *threaten* everything we've been taught—it will simply *widen* it.

There is a difference between destroying something and enhancing it.

Magic enhances perspectives, it doesn't destroy them.

Anything organic gets this. It's why we adapt and evolve. Anything mechanical, however, can't comprehend this—it's too rigid and inflexible to expand. So it shuts the magic down or deems it to be ineffective, unproductive, and not worthy of our consideration or time.

The gift of our times—with all those burning houses—is that our traditional resources have been exhausted, and the conventional tactics of "the way" are no longer enough. As a result, more of us are opening to this "other way," that unexplored wing of human existence that gives us access to entirely new and different possibilities.

It's why I openly call myself a witch.

Calling myself a witch sends out a flare into the nighttime sky that acts like a signal to alert others to my openness to this other way. It also prepares the palette for a taste of something that will break from conventional thought. It's an invitation to go rogue and take a walk on the wild side with me.

Yes, I'm making "witch" synonymous with "leader" here and with a great deal of intention. Plenty of women died because of that moniker, so it's high time we dusted it off.

Because when a woman is fully in her power, she is whole and using everything she's got — *the* way, her way, and everything in between.

She is perfectly capable of logic and thinking far out ahead, planning for every contingency, and can rock an Excel spreadsheet and coordinate legions of people in a syncopated and systematic manner.

AND, left to her own devices, she also knows her body has a built-in GPS that is capable of conjuring and casting spells with her words as a means to guide her and others.

She is trained in logic and mechanics.
She is built for magic and conjuring.

She knows about the plural ways.

She is capable of walking on the floor *and* the ceiling.
And she knows her ornaments will hang on both her boughs and her roots really beautifully.

If she chooses…to know, that is. And remember.
That last bit is key, by the way. It's all up to her.

A woman needs to decide for herself that she has this power within her.

Which can be a big decision for a woman to make because we have a long and ugly history with what happens next in these cases — we just don't use stakes anymore.

To be clear, this is not simply about men not being comfortable with magic and women's power.

What I'm pointing to here is *women* not being comfortable with women's power. Women's resistance to our own power. The patriarchy has trained us all really well, so this discomfort has our fingerprints on it, too.

It's brave as fuck for a woman to *reveal* that much power, let alone *lead* with it.

Because to decide to believe in that other way is to break rank, to go rogue, and to unapologetically embody a woman fully in her power.

To claim this publicly as a leader is to stand out.
To stand out is to be seen.
To be seen is to assume responsibility.
And to assume responsibility is to be held accountable.
To be held accountable is to face the consequences.

Consequences can be dangerous for a woman fully in her power.
They can also be liberating as hell.
And transformational.
And revolutionary.
And medicine.

What I know for sure:

✓ If we women continue to laugh, giggle, mock, roll our eyes, and diminish what we are tapping into when we speak of magic or this other way of moving through life, we will be actively feeding that which we are trying to dismantle: the systemic diminishment of the power of the feminine. It might take some practice and certainly some courage, but holding reverent and public space for this is women's work right now. Much like the naked woman on the boat, we have the power to shift our culture, but women must go first.

✓ Following this other way will at times feel like "cheating" because it feels so natural and easy. Remember, we operate in a culture that values hard struggle and sweat, so to honor this other way is to draw attention to yourself, which might leave you feeling vulnerable or self-conscious. Know that this is not you but a sign of our culture seeking to pull you back into line.

✓ In order to move forward faster together, we need to be talking more openly and publicly about magic, feminine power, mystical arts, and alternative approaches and methodologies. Be generous with your sharing and be mindful of underestimating our capacity to accept what you're sharing. It's common to have that concern you might "freak people out" or that they "can't handle" you. Often in these moments, the opportunity arises to reckon with the power you're tapping into within yourself — if *you* can handle *you*.

What helps:

✓ Get in your body however you can: take a hot bath, put

on some funky music and move your hips, let down your hair, put on some essential oils, rub them in your hands and inhale deeply, light a candle, give yourself a foot massage, roll down the windows of your car and sing loudly. Whatever it takes, and however it looks, the fastest and most effective way for a woman to access her magic is to get in her body.

✓ Go out into nature. Anywhere outside a building or car will do, even if you live in New York City. Seek out *green* space, but in the event that's not an option, just seek out *open* space, as it will immediately cause you to sync with a slower rhythm and deepen your breath. And when your breath goes deeper into your body, you start to plug into your womb space, that source of creation where the divine lives within women. If you're feeling bold, go to the park and hug as many trees as you can find—go "all in" on them. Choose to take the long way home and watch for serendipity to show up. If time is tight, stop to smell the roses and pat a dog.

✓ Gather your women. Or simply call a friend and tell her you love her and were thinking about her. There is a bond between women that is like a golden thread. It glows brighter when we come near each other and has the power to light up even the darkest nights of our soul.

Resources for now or later:

✓ *Waking The Witch : Reflections on Women, Magic, and Power* by Pam Grossman
✓ *Women Who Run with the Wolves* by Clarissa Pinkola Estes
✓ *Wild Mercy* by Mirabai Starr

+ *Witches of Eastwick,* movie

7

"The women are the ones who have always been the midwives and the death doulas. We're quite comfortable with the messy margins of things. We're okay with ambiguity. We don't need to have easy answers, in fact, we're suspicious of them."
—Mirabai Starr—

Threshold

One of my clients, who happened to be a therapist, once gifted me with this perfect word — *liminal* — to describe the geography of *I don't know*, a place I and most of my clients visit often on our quest to find the wellspring.

Apparently, this is the space of psychological transition that clinical practitioners often work in with their clients. It is neither here nor there, which creates tremendous anxiety for Western minds that have been trained to seek out form, function, and logic.

I've come to see liminal space as being a threshold — that piece of horizontal wood that lives in doorways, serving as a transition between two different rooms and providing both a buffer (lest our feet get splinters) and a delineation (visually creating a break in pattern space to space).

I never used to notice thresholds before. I just walked blithely over them, sometimes never even noticing I was moving from one room to another.

That is, until one day my husband, fortified by a particularly strong pot of high-test coffee, announced one bleak Saturday morning in March, "That's it! I'm so tired of looking at that rotting threshold..."

Threshold? What's that?

He brought me to the edge of our kitchen and pointed down at this piece of wood that lay horizontally across the division between the hardwood floor where our kitchen ended and the tile of our mudroom began. The piece of wood I had apparently been living with for over ten years but had never actually noticed until this morning.

It was ugly, that piece of wood. Our house is old, really old, actually, and I marveled that this piece of wood might have been hanging out there serving a *very* important purpose but *completely* without recognition or care since 1929 when it was nailed in.

Eighty years this thing had been walked over.

No wonder it looked so beat to shit.

And now that I was staring at it, I wondered how I could have ever missed it. You know when you see something for the first time that has been there all along? And then you become completely obsessed with it, and then it becomes the only thing you can see? That was my husband that Saturday morning. And he was done.

That morning he ripped up that eighty-year-old piece of tired wood and put down a young whippersnapper piece of maple in its place. And I've never taken thresholds for granted since.

Every time I step over that smooth piece of maple in our home with my bare feet, I take a moment — a pause to feel the hump of it fit snuggly into the arch of my foot *just so* — and I smile. Because I see it. I feel it. I deeply appreciate the purpose it is serving.

I smile all these years later, realizing that this is what my office and my work essentially offer women — a threshold, a smooth piece of maple that feels good to rest upon before crossing over to another room.

This is the space of being neither here nor there. This is the place that exists between knowing and not knowing. This is the time when *I don't know* shows up and is a frequent visitor, like a lonely neighbor who keeps stopping by to chat.

This is why I've gathered us women here on the beach to have this conversation about leading.

Here we are, on this thin and ever-changing strip of sand between the burning houses further inland and the dark ocean out there that's unknown—a threshold between where we've been and where we're headed.

We have not really left the shore, but we're still not heading out into the water.

We're right here, in transition. No longer waiting to take action, but also not really doing anything active.

That's because this is the place of presence, not of doing.

Thresholds are the birthplaces of conscious movement. This is where we arrive before we begin.

It's not comfortable being here, as I'm sure you know.

I mean, think about it…imagine how awkward and self-conscious you might feel hanging out on a threshold, which is essentially a five-inch piece of wood no longer than three feet.

Now imagine hanging out there while other people walk through that same door without a second thought, much as I did for the first ten years of hanging out in our home. And these people, they say:

What are you doing here?
Why are you just standing there?
Can you just move—you're in my way!
I can't shut the door—are you coming or going?
Just make a decision!
Hurry up!
What's your problem?

The ability to stand on thresholds is so important to leading.

Why? Because this is the place of gathering, garnering, and mustering. This is where we are asked to reckon with and take stock of *all* that we don't know, which means this is the place of *humility* and, ultimately, our *humanity*.

It's a really, really important place, even as it's hard, because we're no longer confined by the box we just broke out of, but we're still opening ourselves to what we're moving toward.

This is the place not of waiting but of reverent pause. All that is required of us here is our humble presence.

And it seems it's something I'm good at because it's where I meet my clients time and time again, each of us perched on a thin strip of maple that's no longer here, but not quite there.

It's right here. Asking us to honor it, however hard.

I look at this woman I'm working with, and I hear her saying she doesn't know. I believe her. I honor this about her, and yet there is always a part of me that also trusts that somewhere deep inside herself, she knows she *does* know.

After all, she's paid a hefty price to sit here with me, an investment in both time and money in herself, even in the face of doubt (*Will this be worth it?*), fear (*Oh shit, something will change as a result of this…*), guilt (*I'm being selfish…I should just be satisfied where I am…*), and uncertainty (*What if I'm not any happier than I am now?*).

So even as she's saying she doesn't know, something in this woman ceases to buy that excuse anymore. Because not knowing has gotten old for her, and she's willing to force her hand a bit, to call her own bluff.

Did you catch that moment she had with herself?

Nothing has changed and yet everything has changed. That is the power of a threshold at work.

I love this woman. I totally get her. Because I *am* her.

She's sitting over there *knowing* I don't have answers for her. She's not looking to me for the six secrets to her success or the twelve steps to get where she wants to go, or the five winning strategies that will move her in the "right" direction.

She knows that I am not her savior, nor am I the guru she's been looking for. She's not looking for me to give her any of my power because she knows we've both got enough of our own.

She knows she is her own holy grail, but her cup feels empty with the unknown.

"I don't even know where to begin. My mind is just drawing a blank," she says.

I look at this woman sitting across from me, and she has that look of a deer, frozen and standing in the middle of the road in the bright high beams of an oncoming car.

She looks paralyzed.
Overwhelmed.
Stuck.
Her eyes are wide.
Filled with tears.

She's sitting over there saying she doesn't know, and I believe her. And yet I can feel the heat of the ember she's got buried somewhere deep inside her belly.

Her desire, nearly smothered to death by her fear.

This is what brave looks like.

And it generally brings us to our knees — or the floor.

Brave women know this floor, and they also know it's not a one-time deal. It's a lifetime lesson of learning how to give in to it, and then get off of it.

And if that's not leadership competency, I don't know what is.

It's also the hallmark of the creative — the poet, the artist, the musician — and the mystic because it intersects so deeply with the divine and a desire to be of service to it and to humanity.

I believe it's called "humility."

And we could use a good dose of this medicine in our world.

But listen to the stories we tell ourselves about the women we admire. We call them fearless, confident, and powerhouses, forgetting that this is only half the picture, the prettiest part of the picture to look at and be with.

In your heart of hearts, you probably know this already, and if given the chance, the main characters in these stories will often be the first to admit that's the case.

It's no secret. It's just something we often don't want to hear because it conflicts with the stories we've been telling ourselves.

Think of Brené Brown lying in a fetal position on the floor of her pantry after being called fat, stupid, and a host of other horrific names when her first TED Talk video went viral.

Think of Elizabeth Gilbert crying on her bathroom floor in the middle of the night, writing feverishly in her notebook for the universe to help her but only being told to go back to bed. Which she did, with tile imprints still fresh on her forehead.

Think of Oprah Winfrey being abused since the age of 9 in rural Mississippi, running away from home at age 13, and getting pregnant and losing the baby a year later at 14.

Think of J.K. Rowling living on state welfare and clinically depressed with a young daughter to support.

Think of Glennon Doyle learning the devastating news of her husband's infidelity the week before her book tour about family and parenting launched.

Think of Julia Child and how lost and aimless she felt in a foreign land, not knowing how to cook until she started to take classes in her late 30s.

Think of Katherine Johnson being driven 120 miles in rural West Virginia so she would find a school that would teach mathematics to an African-American girl.

These are just a few examples, surely, but you get my point. All highly accomplished women have been on the floor of their lives, perched precariously on a threshold that was neither here nor there.

Not as easy, lucky, or charmed as our stories would suggest, right?

I fall into this trap myself, sometimes consciously, because it gives me permission to stay where I am, to play small, instead of venturing out into the unknown

In those brief moments — or lifetimes — when we believe in the truth of the stories we tell ourselves about women who lead and who succeed, we can see them as *special* and *different* from us.

Which means we have an ironclad reason to stay safely where we are, ensconced in our bubbles of excuses, half-truths, and misperceptions about what we might be capable of if we were to go for it.

So, these stories we tell ourselves? They're convenient excuses for our fears to gain a foothold. They are the heavy blankets that quickly smother our dreams before they can ignite. They are the funhouse mirrors that distort our perceptions of ourselves.

Threshold moments happen when women tap into and create from a deeper place of resourcefulness.

Because she's found the wellspring, and it's beginning to flow and fill her up with wisdom that will soon become knowledge.

Another of my clients was at this place, too, and it was like seeing a switch being thrown in her.

This woman was a single working mom who was solely responsible for the care of her child. She had just made it through a really long, nasty, and expensive divorce and was starting to feel hope again now that she wasn't fighting for her life.

When she looked around, she suddenly realized how bored she was, uninspired by what she was doing in her 9-5 work-a-day, and wondering if there was something more for her "out there." You know, on the other side of where she was.

We talked about it hypothetically to let some oxygen of possibility enter into the conversation, and I asked her: "So what would you do if you got fired today?"

And I heard her grin — all the way over the phone lines from the deep South — as she responded:

That's easy: I'd get my hustle on.

This is the place behind the veil where a *lot* of shit goes down that *doesn't* get talked about openly on social media or get acknowledged at dinner parties. This is all the "on the way" stuff that's lost in the wake of our fixation on finally arriving "there."

This is the energetic place of road trips and what-the-fuck moments and holy-shit-am-I-allowed-to-want-that forays. This is the barefoot place where give-a-shit meters give way to unspoken desires fueled by bigger reserves of inner resourcefulness.

This is where the land around us starts to feel a bit more expansive and freer, allowing us to see more clearly and notice things we might not have seen before.

This is where "knowing" gives way to saucier and more barefoot words like *hustle* and *parlay* and *badassery*, and we use words like *pluck, moxie, chops, flinty, gumption, scrappy, and chutzpah* to describe these women.

This is also where we show up to this conversation with ourselves with a can of Red Bull in one hand and a machete in the other.

Are you seeing that playful spirit and sense of adventure move in where fear was before?

That's the power of a threshold. It plugs you into the motherboard and fills you up.

Imagine you're like one of the contestants on *The Amazing Race*, and you've just traveled halfway around the world and have no idea where you are in relation to any of the other contenders. Does it matter? You're on an adventure!

Having landed in the foreign land thoroughly exhausted but still vibrating with anticipation, and not sure where—or if—you'll be headed on your next leg of the journey, you run up to that big official *Amazing Race* mat and stand firmly on it, ready to reckon with what you receive from the host.

And then you step off the mat and get your hustle on.

What I know for sure:

✓ We are taught to freeze and stay perfectly still in transition —
think of a deer in the headlights — as if that will keep us
safe or somehow help us. What it *actually* does is paralyze
our system at the very time we are seeking to be present
to what's there for us. It freezes us when we most need
flow from the wellspring to find us. We are not dragonflies
trapped in amber or a specimen trapped between two
panes of glass. Be present, but watch for feeling frozen.

✓ Our society likes things neat and tidy, so when one of
us goes rogue it disturbs the entire ecosystem. It can
trigger bullet-like questions: *What you're doing? Why are
you doing it? Where are you going? Are you sure you know
what you're doing? Do you need help?* Sometimes it can feel
like judgment and other times it can feel like concern, but
know that none of it is yours to own — it's the noise of the
system you're in trying to make sense of something that's
been disrupted.

✓ Transition is messy business, and it can be loud. You might
whine, moan, complain, cry, or wail. It's not a graceful or
serene time, it just isn't. Think of a woman in labor when
the baby is neither out nor is it fully in — that "crowning"
moment when she is opened the widest. Yeah, that. Only
instead of a baby coming out, envision the wellspring
flowing in. These moments warrant a bejeweled crown, so
it's important to love up on yourself here. It's brave and
bold to wear that crown.

What helps:

✓ See if you can get yourself near or in a body of water. A bath will do in a pinch, but an ocean is ideal. The expansiveness of the sea and the sounds and currents of the water will offset the constriction you might be feeling from being in a threshold moment. Water works magic on women.

✓ Plug into the motherboard. Find a patch of garden or a discrete corner of a public park, take off your shoes, and sink your feet into the dirt. If it's winter outside, stick your hands in the soil of a potted plant. This is called "earthing" and is amazingly restorative medicine for when you're feeling disconnected and disoriented.

✓ Name what you're feeling. You don't need to make it a big hairy ordeal or even understand it, and you definitely don't have to *do* anything with it. But name each and every thing you're feeling. Make a pile: *like a fraud, embarrassed, worried, ashamed, overwhelmed, anxious, self-conscious....* Rumi talks about this in his poem "The Guest House," greeting each visitor at the door laughing. Just keep naming and piling until you feel a small smile forming on your lips.

Resources for now or later:

✓ *Outrageous Openness: Letting the Divine Take the Lead* by Tosha Silver
✓ *Feminine Genius* by LiYana Silver
✓ *Foxfire, Wolfskin and Other Stories of Shapeshifting Women* by Sharon Blackie

+ *A Wrinkle in Time* by Madeleine L'Engle (or movie)

8

*"What we need now is for more women
to ride their chariots of love into the center of town."*
—Elizabeth Lesser—

The Almighty Point

"What is your heartbreak?" she asked.

Seriously? That's a downer of a question, I thought. I squirmed in my seat a little in the darkened theatre that day, hoping no one would notice me scoffing at how *that* was remotely relevant to me.

But damn, if she didn't hold the silence in that moment before launching into her story in front of the audience at the Business Innovation Factory's annual summit.

Angela Maiers went on to tell us that each and every one of us mattered, and she shared how she had been using this very question to engage the minds and hearts of kids from kindergarten to high school to plug them into their power to affect change in the world. Helping them to see more clearly how they *could* and therefore *did* matter.

My brain wasn't scoffing anymore. It had data now, and I leaned in a bit as if the judge on the bench had just raised a bushy eyebrow of skepticism but then surprised us all by saying, "Proceed...."

My heartbreak....my heartbreak....my mind sought to be helpful, as if patting its coat pockets looking for the keys.

Where did I last put my heartbreak? I know I stashed it somewhere safe, so I wouldn't lose it...

But my heart was already there, two steps ahead, offering me the image of the US presidential chart, of all things. You know, the one hung in all the elementary schools in this country that lists all the white guys who have led our nation, plus one black man whose race and citizenship have always been under attack?

Yeah, that one.

The fact that my children have grown up seeing (essentially) the same poster of presidents that I saw growing up — 45 years ago? Well now, that just broke my heart, that image.

My heart wasn't just broken, it was ripped open.

Sorrow intersected with rage and collided with desire as I sat in that dark theatre. I'm fairly certain visible smoke was coming out of my ears as tears streamed down my cheeks.

But like a muscle after a good workout, I could feel that the rip wasn't life-threatening. In fact, it was igniting a fire in me, sparking life.

That was the moment I began to see myself as a leader of leaders. I didn't want to just make a living supporting women trying to move up in (or out of) organizations.

I wanted to be part of a revolution of change led by women.

I felt it kindle in me recently on a trip to London. It was my boys' first trip to Europe, something we had not planned but sort of happily fell into when a hurricane wiped out the plans I had made to take my family on a vacation to celebrate my 50th birthday.

We marked the occasion with the highlight of the trip, seeing a production of *Les Mis* in the West End. They had never before seen a show like this, and I was so excited to introduce them to it.

What I wasn't prepared for were the tears as a fire reignited in my belly that night.

I sat between the two of them (it was my birthday!) as the house lights came down, and I felt the tears as something in my bones remembered what *Les Mis* was designed to do: ignite.

I hadn't seen this play since I was 19 years old — 31 years in my past. And now, as I sat in that darkened theatre with my hands resting on the knees of my sons, I heard the song inviting us to join in the crusade by letting the beating our hearts match the beating of the drum, and I was moved to tears. I lit up inside with a desire to be part of a revolution, to lead the charge, to stand up high on the barricade and call for change.

My sons know me well and were so kind to bear witness to me that day in the dark (it was my birthday!). I swear they must have had bruises of their legs as my gentle hand turned into a pounding thump, which made the tears flow even more because I knew they believed in me.

They saw me as the leader I am.

Later, I would receive a card from my eldest telling me that he hoped he would someday make as much impact on the world as he saw me making, which just about slayed me (in a good way).

But that night in the theatre, I could feel myself enlisting them as much as I could feel myself enlisting me, albeit with a slight modification to better suit our times.

And here I thought Angela's question was just a stupid icebreaker exercise. That question was everything.

My heartbreak was the point, and I was now hell-bent on sharpening it by the fire that had been lit in me that day.

It's like that beautiful scene in the movie *The Secret Life of Walter Mitty* when Ben Stiller's character reckons with the path not taken and is beckoned to take it by the image of the adventure photographer played by Sean Penn. At the time, he's working in the basement of *Life* magazine and is keenly aware of the irony in how he's not honoring magazine's motto:

> *To see the world, to come to things dangerous*
> *To see behind walls, to draw closer*
> *To find each other, and to feel*
> *That is the purpose of Life.*

Like Walter Mitty, I wanted to see what was beyond the barricades, but I felt like I was holding myself hostage in a basement of my own making, envious of those "out there" who were living the adventure.

So, on the day I heard Angela speak, I was quick to seek her out during intermission to thank her for her story, but when I finally got to the front of the line of people who had that same idea, she looked right at me and said:

"Oh, you're SheChanges! You're Lael!"

I had never met this woman before, and she—SHE—had been the one on stage, not me. I was the shifty, skeptical one in the dark, remember?

But she knew me from social media and was familiar with my work. She was wonderfully gracious, and I soon recovered my senses, but that moment lodged itself in my bones for safekeeping.

How did I not see myself as she did? Why did I show up dim, blinded by her light?

I knew better than that.

But, you see, I did that thing we are trained to do so well as women. I compared myself to her.

She was on stage, I was not. She was all put together and professional, and I was just pretending, trying hard not to feel like a fraud hanging out among these cool people.

She had a slick and memorable elevator pitch, and I was still bumbling my way through explaining what it is I do...exactly.

She memorized—and crushed—a twenty-minute story, and I needed notecards for a five-minute one.

And on and on and on... My brain filled in all these story holes about this woman I'd never met, and I came up seriously lacking by comparison, so I snuffed myself out before someone else would.

This is what happens when your head engages in mortal combat with your heart.

Things get ugly and mean, like two junkyard dogs attacking each other, yanking their cinderblock chains this way and that, until a cold hose comes out, leaving them both soaked, embarrassed, and still pissed.

That sort of shit has you think twice before you ever allow your heart fire to be ignited again, let me tell you.

I see and hear my clients' junkyard dogs go at it and yank at those same damn chains every day.

"What's the point of doing it if it's not good?"

I hear that question so often from clients. Hell, I *ask* that question so often myself. So, I can appreciate firsthand how every slight detour or deviation from our "normal" day-to-day operations are often met with an elaborate vetting system with plenty of checks and balances and hoops to jump through to even give ourselves permission to do it.

At which point, we're so thoroughly exhausted from the Robert's Rules of Order in our head, we've long since checked out and given up and crawled deep under the pile of other words that take the fizz out of our ginger ale, like "pragmatic," "productive," "valuable," "good enough," "worth it," or, my personal favorite, "prudent."

These are all words designated to get us "back on track" (whose track that is, exactly, can be a whole other conversation).

Bottom line: We're off it, be it a track, a rocker, or a point.

So on that day, when my client asked herself that question, *"What's the point?"* we paused. Rather than barreling through with the assumption that there *was* a point, we actually spent some time actually considering that question from a place of curiosity, rather than judgment.

She had been trying to carve out some time in her busy life to feed her creativity, deciding that painting was something that she wanted to do more. Except she wasn't doing it.

It was clear she was hitting something—resistance, fear, overwhelm, or some concoction of all three—and when I extrapolated her specific experience across the all the similar questions I've heard from women over the years, it starts to sound something like this:

What's the point of making art if it's not good?
What's the point of writing if no one reads it?
What's the point of making music if no one hears it?
What's the point of gardening if the plants are just going to die?
What's the point of fighting for change if there's always someone who is going to disagree with you?
What's the point of trying something new if you don't have time to master it?
What's the point of slowing down if you will have a pile of work waiting for you when you return?
What's the point of fresh-cut flowers by your bed if you won't see them when you sleep?
What's the point of romance and intimacy if you don't have a partner?
What's the point of sending a handwritten thank-you note, if it's faster just to send a text or an email?
What's the point of giving something if you don't get credit for it?
What's the point of having a business if you don't grow it?
What's the point of crying if it doesn't change anything?

What IS the point?

This is the voice we answer to in our society.
This is what keeps us in our heads, keeps us up at night, keeps us from trying anything new, scary, or different.
This is the voice that accuses us of "wasting" our time.

This is the judge we plead our cases before when it comes to allowing desire, pleasure, joy, beauty, play, stillness, the natural world, intimacy, our emotions, or our truth take center stage.

This is the voice that determines what is worthy of our time.

Do you see what I'm getting at? We've lost our way. Ironically, we've missed the point in our feverish attempts to stick the landing.

We've let our heartbreaks bleed out— sometimes to death—instead of honoring them for what they are: a heart fire ignited.

And yet our hearts keep beating, and our desire, it just. Keeps. Rising.

We've lost our way because of our love of the destination, forward progress, the outcome, and the return on our investment.

We've lost our way because we can't imagine a world beyond the barricades we've built.

We've forgotten that lines aren't the only forms we humans can make. And that there are more crayons for us to color with other than black and white and a few shades of gray.

Women will help us to see beyond the barricades.

They will remind us how we can curve and bend. We can wax and wane. We can ebb and flow. We can rise and set. We can wander and not be lost. We can be present and moving. We can be still and active. We can bleed and not die. We can be silent and engaged.

Women will remind us because this is their native soil they've lived on for lifetimes — silently, privately, often hidden from view, in order to survive in a society built on the opposite values.

As the guardians of the wellspring, women are getting more ferocious in their devotion to it because once they have lost and then found their way back to it, they remember enough for us all.

We are designed to have curves, even as we live in a world that favors lines.

We are designed to have cycles, even as we move in a society that asks us to run like machines.

We are designed to bleed regularly and not die, even as our bodies are disparaged, dishonored, and violated.

We are designed to be inconsistent, even though we are trained that steady, regular, modulated movement is best.

We are designed to see webs of interconnectedness, even as we exist within a culture that seeks to actively divide us.

We are designed to create new life inside ourselves, even though it is viewed as inconvenient, disruptive, burdensome, and unmentionable.

Maybe that's the point: the massive power we hold as women.

And yet our heads continue to pummel us with questions — it's just what heads do.

In the case of my client, she wanted to know:

Where am I going with this?

Why does this matter?
How will this help anything?
How is this not a waste of my time?
What if nothing changes as a result?
What if I suck and people laugh?
What if I'm good and I really am an artist?
What if I can't stop?
What if I don't ever want to stop?
What if it makes me cry?
Then what do I do?
What happens next?

Our poor, tired heads…they work so damn hard for us, don't they?

But here's the point, beautiful heads:

We've forgotten the **power** and **pleasure** that comes from actively engaging our senses. And that is critical because it brings color and vitality into a world that has drained so much of it from our people.

We've forgotten what **rapture** and **presence** feel like. And that is critical to our humanity because it connects us to hope, each other, and this big, beautiful, blue-green planet we share.

We've forgotten how to **live from our bodies.**

And that is critical because so many of us are sick and tired, and something's gotta give at a time when many of us feel like we've got nothing left to offer.

What if it were the other way around?

What if we lived in a world where the value system was flipped, and the "point" didn't really matter? What if we didn't give away so much damn power to the point? What if the joy, happiness, or fulfillment we're seeking weren't dependent on being seen, heard, bought, or applauded?

Because if art imitates life, then maybe the opposite is true, which would position the artists among us as leaders.

Let me ask you this: What makes an artist an artist? The number of hours she dedicates to her craft? The school where she studied? The number of pieces sold? When her art is able to support her financially? When she gets her own show?

We have conversations like this a lot in my family, probably because I was an art major in college and can get a bit prickly about it. One of my boys will point out a minimalist painting in a museum with, say, a simple white square in the center of a white canvas and say, "How is that art? I could have made that..."

And then before I can say anything, the other will jump in and say, "I know what you're going to say, Mom.... 'Yeah, but you *didn't* make that.'"

They know me well, apparently.

An artist is an artist when she says yes to what's inside her.

Could the same be true for being a leader?

What if it wasn't about your title, your credibility, or electability (or any ability), your experience, where you went to school, who you know, how many likes or followers you have, the color of your skin, or if you "look" like a leader?

It might *be* about all that. It just wouldn't be *because* of all that.

This isn't about our beautiful heads at all. It's about consistently and fiercely feeding the fire that lives in our hearts.

What kind of world would we live in if we could all set our hearts on fire?

I believe women will show us how if we follow their lead.

But it will require us working together as we never have before — and getting fierce about it, maybe even pissing people off who have a vested interest in our *not* banding together.

Maybe even making art like our lives depended on it.

What I know for sure:

✓ At its core, this chapter is an invitation to examine our current relationships to pleasure, time, and productivity. To move beyond the ordered "way it is" within our minds, we must strike out into the messy margins and blank canvas of the unknown, which is where we will discover what matters most to us and our world.

✓ Presence requires us to move more slowly, and even stop, which is a radical act in a society that values speed, productivity, and destination. One of the best ways to strengthen this muscle is to get off the beaten path of familiarity, maybe even allow yourself to get lost. As we do when traveling in a foreign land, the invitation is to let your senses help you navigate and make meaning of what's around you, bringing you fully present to "what's here now" as opposed to preoccupied with "where you're headed."

✓ There's something that happens for women when we give ourselves the permission and the space to create. We remember our resourcefulness to figure shit out, we allow it to be messy, unfinished, and "just for fun" — which we then apply to our lives as a whole. We play with color, we use our hands, and feel our way with our hearts, which help us to see outside the black-and-white boxes of our minds. We smile, laugh, and feel a sense of satisfaction from making something out of nothing, which helps us to reconnect with the power we hold in our bodies every day.

What helps:

✓ Make a trip to your favorite craft or art store and get some fresh supplies for whatever you fancy—pastels, acrylics, charcoals, felt, fabrics, beads—and see where it takes you.

Sign up for a class with a friend to learn that thing you've been wanting to learn — knitting, woodworking, pottery. Give yourself permission to suck and be a beginner at something, so you can remember what it feels like. When all else fails, play in the dirt, make a snowman, or build a sandcastle.

✓ Throw down a creative gauntlet for yourself and watch how you rise to meet the challenge. Make it audacious and bat-shit-crazy ambitious, but look for how it lights you up with permission to actually do it. Set up some structure and accountability. Enlist in an online community, organize your friends, or announce your intentions publicly — to build a treehouse, write a book, hold an art show — and set a date for people to come see it...before you start.

✓ Host a dinner party with your favorite people for no particular reason. Be overt about the pleasure it gives you. Take your time anticipating it, savoring the possibilities, paging through cookbooks, and imagining rituals that would make it feel special. Make it a feast for your senses — string lights or use candles, have fresh flowers or set a table in the garden, use linens or a picnic blanket, listen to a playlist or live drumming. Take your sweet time, dress for the occasion, and treat yourself extra special as the host with a massage or a pedicure beforehand. Be present to the event long before it actually happens. Let it build slllooowwwllly.

Resources for now or later:

✓ Elizabeth Gilbert's *Magic Lessons* Podcast interview with Brené Brown (episode #12)
✓ *The Artist's Way* by Julia Cameron (try her Morning Pages)
✓ *My Kitchen Year* by Ruth Reichl

+ *Under the Tuscan Sun*, movie

Roots

What's Happening to Me?

IMAGINE you're minding your own business walking down a crowded city street, and suddenly you feel the ground vibrating beneath your feet. You stop, unsure of what you've just felt, and ask a fellow pedestrian, "What was THAT!?"

Distracted, the person glances quickly over at you and says, "What was WHAT?" You dismiss it, thinking you must have imagined something, and then you feel it again…and again…and again. Until you can no longer deny that something is happening, even though no one seems to notice and nothing is making sense.

That is the best way I can think of to describe this sensation of when your roots start talking to you. This is how it feels when change wants to come and is asking you to take the lead to make that happen. Far from a lightning bolt of inspiration (coming down from on high), it often begins from somewhere deep down in our bodies (coming from down low…), where they connect with the earth. It's subtle, until it's unmistakably there.

Which is why it's so easy to miss…until it's not.

This is the place where we feel the most…off (off track, off-kilter, off our rocker, off-script), and go inward to see if we can sort it all out and make sense of it under cover of darkness. "Feel" is the operative word here as it tends to start with an emotion bubbling up in our bodies, even before we can put words to it. And because no one else is in your skin and can't see or sense or understand what you're feeling, this is also the place where we feel most alone. This is where difficult and dark things find us, like vulnerability, shame, insecurity, guilt, and anger.

Conversely, this is also where we can start to feel most awake and inspired, like we've come out of a stupor and are starting to connect to something bigger than ourselves. Something that matters.

Some of us start to utter phrases we've never used in our lives… like "soul whispers" and "in my bones" and "warrior's path" or "deeply of service." Even the most cynical non-believers among us are amazed by how drawn they are to this conversation that's coming up from inside them because it feels strangely familiar and therefore magnetic.

Time starts ticking loudly in our ears, and there is this weird sense of urgency that rises up through our consciousness, making us use phrases like "life is short" and "now is the time" and "just do it." But here is what I know for sure: While we're sitting in the fog wondering, "Time for *what*? Do *what*, exactly? we are being fueled by something bigger and deeper than what lives in our heads.

9

We cannot expect to change what's in the world
unless we first awaken to what lies deeply within."
—Tererai Trent—

Keening

My nature is electrical. In fact, someone once said working with me was like bumping up against a live wire. "In a good way," she said. I'm all bright eyes, wagging body, and let's-get-this-party-started energy.

But I had this experience once that stopped me in my tracks. And in that moment, I felt like I'd dropped into a completely different arena. Like Katniss Everdeen arriving up through that narrow elevator into the arena of her second Hunger Games, it felt foreign to me but also like it would soon become a home that I'd know intimately.

I can't remember how it began or where it came from, which is often the sign I've been delivered something straight from the Divine.

All I remember is how I felt.

A client of mine describes this feeling as getting "full-body shivers," and I'd agree. It's the sort of sensation that makes you stop — almost like when the hair on your neck stands up when lightning is near. Except your instincts in this case are not to seek cover, they're to get really still and ready to receive.

Somehow, I'd ended up on my phone watching a photographer somewhere in Scandinavia do something I'd never seen before, and once I saw it, I could *not* stop thinking about it.

It's called *kulning*, and apparently, it's an ancient practice of singing high-pitched atonal notes in the middle of a field to draw animals to you.

I shit you not, it's the coolest thing ever. (Google Jonna Jinton kulning, and you'll see...)

In one video, you think nothing is really happening, and then you'll see this cow approaching from out of nowhere....and then another, and another, until this woman is surrounded by a whole herd of cows in the pasture. At which point she laughs as if it's the most natural and fun thing to do in the world.

This woman didn't look like a mystic or a wood sprite or festival-going burner, she was simply a woman standing in a field, photographing to finance her life and kulning to commune with nature.

Time and time again, I watched as this woman stood alone in a field or the woods and made these eerie and mystical noises. You could call it singing, but it doesn't seem fitting as there are no discernable words or melody, and clearly, she is making it up as she goes.

Toning is more like it. Channeling might be going a bit too far.

Needless to say, I was obsessed. What *was* it about this ancient practice that drew me in like a moth to a flame? I could not stop watching YouTube videos of her. *Haunted* best describes what I was feeling, as I began researching what this thing was that I had never heard of before.

That search led me to another practice, this one born out of Celtic roots. It's called *keening*, and it has a very similar quality to kulning, in that it is atonal, doesn't possess lyrics, and is different every time it's sung.

Apparently, keening is an Irish lament, the Gaelic equivalent of the blues, and is generally known to help ease the burden of emotions too difficult to express, such as grief. Indeed, keening is generally known to be associated with funerals and the processions that honor the dead.

Did I happen to mention I was *born* on the day of the dead? And my name is Gaelic?

The magnet in me was growing stronger.

Margaret Bennett, a Celtic singer and songwriter who is often associated with laments, describes keening like this:

"It's kind of paradoxical, because on the one hand, we're not very vocal when it comes to speaking up...we've had a history of that kind of oppression. But when it comes to song, what you can't say, you can often sing."

So why was I obsessively going down rabbit holes researching this, haunted by the non-melodies until all hours of the night?

I didn't know, but clearly something in my woman bones did. Something was happening to me, and I was letting it.

But I soon learned I wasn't alone. I showed it to a friend who came over that week, and we both watched the videos — kulning and keening — entranced, rapt by something we couldn't name, and slack-jawed by how we felt hearing it.

Something in our woman bones was waking up, and we both knew it.

This is how it feels when your roots start speaking to you.

You stop in your tracks, and all your senses come alive, ready to turn toward a subtle snap of a twig underfoot or detect a hidden path that had previously gone unnoticed.

And that's all well and good, but what the hell did this have to do with women leading? With me? I wasn't going to be calling the cows or lamenting over the dead anytime soon in Portland, Maine.

When I thought about it more, though, I started to appreciate that it actually had a lot to do with who I am as a leader—more specifically, what I'm capable of as a leader.

I could sense when things didn't make sense.

Maybe that high-pitched atonal quality women possessed (puts a whole new spin on "shrill," doesn't it?) was a way to commune with the natural world.

As more women find their way back to the wellspring, the source of the feminine and our deepest wisdom, maybe this is a way to communicate with the natural world that lives within it?

What if women could *speak* the language that's spoken behind the veil of things unseen, and we simply hadn't *known* it all these years?

I don't recall that being a choice for a language to learn in my high school curriculum.

My best friend in school used to get in trouble for humming, though. She didn't even realize she was doing it, but I remember it used to drive me crazy. I'd nudge her to stop before she'd get in trouble again, and she'd always look surprised, as if I'd interrupted her in the middle of a trance.

Did I mention her father had died quite suddenly two years before? Maybe she was onto something, even without realizing it. Maybe her body knew how to take her where her heart wanted to go, even while she sat staring out the window in algebra class.

If women are the gatekeepers of the wellspring, then it makes sense we would somehow know how to find our way back. And if we can find our way back, others could follow us.

They could take our lead.

If we could just take it seriously, that is — see it as real and not dismiss it as something crazy, silly, or weird.

Because the truth of it is, women's voices are a powerful force to facilitate both life *and* death. Maybe that explains why midwives and hospice workers are almost always women?

I mentioned keening at funerals, but think of a woman deep in the throes of labor and the noises she makes. What does the midwife (if she's there) typically ask the woman?

"See if you can deepen your voice, like a moan."

Somewhere I learned the biological reason that explains why this works. If you think of your voice as an instrument or a tube that air passes through, it has something to do with high pitches being created by constriction and lower vibrations being created by relaxed muscles.

The *higher* the sound, the more it moves *up* into your body.
The *lower* the sound, the more it moves *down* into your body.

So, the crown chakra (or top of your head) is activated by the high-pitched tone "eeeeee," and the root chakra (sacrum area) is activated by the deeper tone "uummmm."

Both of my boys were born vaginally and were nearly 10 lbs. each, so let me tell you, I was moaning to beat the band, thanks to my midwife's wise counsel. Nothing silly about it, and it was a hell of a lot less invasive than the caesarean the attending doctor was recommending.

But then years later, I would learn another interesting fact about women's voices, this time through a conflux of events that intertwined my studies with Lisa Lister about being a witch.

At the time, I had this vexing problem with my throat that just kept troubling me. I could breathe and swallow just fine, but it felt like I had this constant sensation of a large marble stuck in the back of my throat. I was terrified I had esophageal cancer.

What I know now that I didn't know then is that I was healing some very, very old cellular memory. There was a poster made famous during the Women's March of 2017 that read:

We are the granddaughters of the witches you couldn't burn.

I am one of them, it seems, as my throat was constricting like fury the more I studied about witches and wrote this book about women's power and our distinct ways of leading.

Two things happened from that moment: I initiated myself as a witch, and I got an endoscopy.

"Say your prayers, and tether your camel," as one of my clients is known to say.

The endoscopy came back clear. The kind doctor looked at me after the procedure and said, "You do not have cancer." I sobbed with relief, and then I asked her tentatively (unsure if I'd get what I often get from traditional healers), "Could this be about the book I'm writing?"

She surprised me by leaning in, putting her hand on my arm, and saying, "Absolutely."

Upon further research into the witch world, I soon discovered that—get this—the tissues in women's throats and our cervixes are *exactly* the SAME.

Which means a woman *giving birth* is as powerful as a woman *giving voice.*

A woman's voice is her primary way to express her truth, just as a woman's cervix is her primary way to bring forth life.

No wonder we're scared shitless of both.

The truth is where it's at for women these days (#metoo) with so many women sick and tired of holding it in and biting our tongues. It's serving no one, and we get this.

Writer Chimamanda Ngozi Adichie spoke to this very thing at a commencement address she gave at Harvard in 2018:

"What I know is that I have always felt my best and done my best when I veer toward truth. When I don't lie. And the biggest regrets of my life are those times when I did not have the courage to embrace the truth."

But so often what we have inside us doesn't ever see the light of day. It might show a little if you're really looking for it, but to the naked, untrained eye it remains hidden.

I used to have a cat named Nikki that gave me a perfect visual to describe this. He didn't know it at the time, he was a cat just doing his thing, but years later I would remember fondly.

We always presumed Nikki had a bit of a grudge with the world in general, having been abandoned by the side of a busy road, and also having had to bear the brunt of an unfortunate miscommunication between my mom and the vet that left him without his balls and all of his claws…in the same day.

He was a good cat, and we loved him, even though he was (understandably) disdainful of us and had this weird habit of eating yarn.

We would come home at the end of the day to find Nikki lounging in the sun. We'd stop to give him a pat, and it was only then that we would notice this little bit of red yarn peeking out from the side of his mouth.

Curious, we'd give a little tug, and this little bit of yarn would grow before our eyes until it was clear he had ingested a few yards of the stuff.

(For cat lovers out there: He was fine…it was the 80s, and we didn't worry then like we did now. He died at the age of 15 from a non-yarn-related death. Stay with me.)

I've come to appreciate that noticing that little bit of red, getting curious, and then pulling gently the bit of yarn is kind of like what I do for my living—only with women, not cats. It's that thing I am able to do that I mentioned before, sensing when things don't make sense and listening for what remains unsaid.

At first blush, you think it's one thing, but once you give a little tug, out comes an *entirely* different truth that was apparently hanging out all the way at the end of that long piece of yarn—deep in her gut, away from the light of day.

Talk about swallowing our truth.

And let me tell you, there are *lots and lots* of women out there with little bits of red yarn hanging out of the corner of their mouths right now. Just look for them, they're everywhere.

Here's an example of the three most frequent little bits of red yarn I've witnessed, and what's revealed after we get to the bottom of it:

She'll say: *I don't understand.*
At the bottom of the yarn will be: *I fundamentally disagree.*

She'll say: *I'm not ready.*
At the bottom of the yarn will be: *I'm not enough.*

She'll say: *They're not ready for me.*
At the bottom of the yarn will be: *I'm too much.*

Do you see how that works? What presents as a women's truth is only the tip of her iceberg of truth.

That's on us to own.

What I know for sure:

✓ Our truth can get muffled over time as we get more practiced (and sadly, rewarded) for burying it beneath piles of excuses or watering it down with a river of denial. Sometimes we even forget it's there, acting surprised when it surfaces years later, the same way rocks eventually poke up through the soil. Because our deepest truths, like those rocks, are organic matter that will endure the test of time and the elements. They will not die, despite our best attempts to bury them alive, and will just keep rising up in us.

✓ There are frequencies of communication that our brains can barely comprehend, and we tend to diminish them by calling them *weird, crazy,* or *ridiculous.* This is the world of intuition, serendipity, and magic, and women tap into this world every day without knowing it — generally when we are most depleted, frustrated, or desperate — as a means to get guidance from some data point other than their heads. By sharing our stories about this more broadly and publicly, we can widen that portal of possibility for others to access for themselves.

✓ There is an inextricable link between women's bodies and the natural world. Women possess the ability to commune with animals and trees, and they talk about it more than you might realize. The more they plug into the natural world, the more practiced they become at interpreting its messages, whether it's from encountering an animal or bird in their path or walking among the trees in a forest. Women's truth flows more freely in nature, partly because the noise of our society falls away, but also because they are more open to receiving.

What helps:

✓ Give your voice a workout. Head to the beach or a wide-open area and give yourself permission to yell as loudly as you can. Feel it dissipate into the wind as it's caught outside of you. Experiment with different tones and pitches and notice how your body responds. Find your range again and reconnect with the power of your own voice.

✓ Make eye contact with strangers, colleagues, or your partner and see if you can hold it for longer than might be ordinary or comfortable. Play with listening and "speaking" without the use of words as a means to strengthen the alternative forms of communication activated by our senses like sight and touch.

✓ Get curious about what lives beneath the words you are using in your life. Listen for vague words like *fine, nice, nervous, okay,* and *ready,* and dig a bit deeper into the root of them. Ask: "Is that true? What does that mean, exactly? What am I not saying?" Enlist an ally here as a partner and point out for each other when you are using benign or intentionally vague words to potentially mask something that is living at the truth of what you're experiencing or feeling.

Resources for now or later:

✓ *If Women Rose Rooted* by Sharon Blackie
✓ *12 Truths I've Learned from Life and Writing,* TED Talk by Anne Lamott
✓ *Becoming* by Michelle Obama

+ *Nanette,* a Netflix special by Hannah Gadsby

10

"We have come to be danced.
Not the invisible, self-conscious shuffle,
but the matted hair flying, voodoo mama shaman shakin' ancient bones dance
The strip us from our casings, return our wings, sharpen our claws & tongues dance
The shed dead cells and slip into the luminous skin of love dance..."
—Jewel Mathieson—

Holy Shit

I have this old woman who lives inside me.

She sits by a campfire that I imagine to be right by my solar plexus. She's also the one I constantly forget about, so seeing her each time is like meeting her anew.

She never seems to take it personally, though. It seems she knows that I'll come looking for her eventually. Maybe, like so many women, she's gotten good at waiting.

I first discovered her during a very unlikely moment—or maybe it was the perfect moment because I was feeling rather desperate.

I was at that place where so many of my clients today currently are in, the one that compels them to seek *me* out. Which makes me think that maybe I *am* a flesh-and-bones version of the ancient woman that I know lives inside me.

I was at a place where I knew I needed to leave my corporate job, but I also knew I couldn't afford to leave. Something was clearly trying to come out of me, and for the life of me I couldn't seem to find a way to stuff it back in—and increasingly, I found I didn't want to.

But what was it? And why was it? And how was this all going to go down, exactly?

I wanted those sensations to stop — they were super-inconvenient, highly disruptive to my status quo, and thoroughly overwhelming — and yet something deep inside me was so damn relieved they were there.

I couldn't turn away from it. This was the wellspring bubbling up in me, and it just tasted so… good. Once I got a small sip of it, I was ruined for ordinary tap water.

So, on the way to work that gray March morning in Maine — after dropping off my firstborn at childcare — I swung by the beach and rolled down the car window to let the sound of the waves soothe my weary soul and my fretting head.

I took a deep breath, closed my eyes, and instantly got a clear image of a smoldering fire inside me — like one that you'd find still smoking in the early morning hours after a raging campfire the night before.

Curious, I looked around in my mind's eye and saw an older woman seated by the fire. I almost missed her because of the smoke.

She patted the ground next to her and smiled at me with the most loving expression I'd ever seen — like she had been waiting for me and was delighted that I'd finally come.

She gestured to the fire that was nearly out and nodded, clearly wanting me to blow on the fire to get it started again.

I knew how to blow on a fire to get it started. It's what I now do for my living.

So I blew, slow and steady, down low, where the coals rest on the land. And again, I blew, slow and steady. Until at last, it ignited. I blew some more to ensure it would stay lit, and then I sat back, satisfied with my efforts.

The old woman looked at me and smiled, her eyes filled with love for me. She never did say anything to me that day, nor has she said anything since. I guess she doesn't need to because her sole job seems to be to get me to tend my fire, as simple as that sounds.

The ability to light my own fire is my most direct way back to the wellspring. No one can do it for me.

But sometimes it's so confusing that we don't know — or don't want to know — what to make of it. It just feels...too much.

That was the case when a client told me about her hot lava of love.

"I feel like I have this love just pouring out of me...but I don't know how that relates to anything we've been talking about," she said a bit hesitantly.

This woman had not hired me to talk about love pouring out of her, and I could feel her awareness of that fact as she was talking. She was, by all accounts, a high-powered senior executive who was interested in assuming greater levels of leadership at not only her firm, but also in her industry as a whole.

So, I could see her wondering the same thing Tina Turner used to sing about:

What's love got to do with it?

But the thing is, it wasn't her mind that had grabbed the mic that afternoon in my office, it was her enormous heart that was speaking. Her mind, it seems, wasn't entirely sure what to do about it.

This conversation we were having was coming on the heels of a series of volcanic eruptions — quite literally. Almost all the women in my practice for those few weeks had mentioned the volcanoes in Hawaii and how they could relate to them: overtaking the roadways, causing massive fissures in the earth's crust, bringing everything to a screeching halt with the sheer force of nature.

Women were captivated by these volcanoes.

The thing is, all these women thought they were the only ones who felt *one* with the volcanoes, who identified with them. They didn't realize that from where I sat, it was like of chorus of women saying and feeling the same thing.

Me, too. Me, too. Me, too.

What *does* love have to do with it?

This woman sitting across from me knew the answer to that question without my even asking it because *everything* about her screamed "warrior of love." — She was a wolverine of a mother, a fierce advocate of social justice and environmental protection, a loyal friend, a devoted daughter, and a steadfast partner to both her beloved as well as her firm.

Everything had to do with love, and she knew it, but there was something happening inside her heart that felt a lot like those volcanoes in Hawaii, and she wasn't quite sure what to make of it.

It was like that fierce love inside her had grown too big to be contained by her body, and with each passing day, it was threatening to explode out of her — with or without her permission — demanding to be expressed, heard, and seen more globally.

That love lava in her wanted to be of greater service and have more impact.

But what's an executive swollen with love to do? Where do you go with all that hot lava before it wreaks havoc on a thoughtfully designed life that didn't factor that in?

Dr. Tererai Trent has a lot of thoughts about that in her book *The Awakened Woman*. She shares her own incredible story of being a young, single mother of four, without a job, without an education, and living in poverty in her village in Zimbabwe, to getting her Ph.D., living with her family in the United States, and ultimately starting her own foundation to build schools for girls.

She talks and writes about women's ability to plug into The Greater Good, a concept that reminds me of what waits for us all in the wellspring, that groundwater that connects us to each other and to our planet.

The place where deep service intersects with fierce leadership.

It's the place where we snap out of our stupor, wake ourselves up, and in the process wake up others around us.

That's what I believe women are doing in our world right now.

Waking us the fuck up. With love.

One of my clients shared a story about how she did this. She was at the funeral for her son and was supposed to be acting a certain way — or so it was presumed.

She was supposed to be quiet and drowning in her emotions and mute because she had no words. She was supposed to be exhausted, depleted, and void of her life source. And in fact, there were moments in her grieving process when she was all of that, but not that day.

She decided to use her moment of grief to serve our greater good.

On the day of the funeral, she walked up to the front and grabbed two sticks and started to WHACK them loudly together above her head, a wild look in her eyes as she met the gazes around the room.

She wasn't talking as much as she was embodying her talk. WAKE UP, her actions said. BE HERE NOW, each loud smack of the wood conveyed. LIVE LIFE TODAY, she exuded.

Far from jarring the crowd that had gathered, her actions did something else instead: They woke them up. She called them to attention. She became a focal point when the stupor was threatening to overtake them.

Their response? Deep gratitude. People came up to her afterward and thanked her for what she had done, saying it had stirred something inside them that had gone dormant. Mourners approached her saying they felt energized, inspired, and more committed than they had in a while.

She wasn't too much. She was of service.

They had gathered around death and had surprisingly discovered life. All because of this woman no one saw coming. She blindsided them with her service.

How often do we not see *her* coming?

147

How often are *we* that woman that wants to grab the sticks but instead sit on our hands, acting like we're supposed to act, not wanting to bother people with our noise?

How often do we contribute to our collective stupor?

This woman didn't choreograph this to be dramatic and hadn't really spent a lot of time thinking about it. She was a mother grieving the death of her son.

What she did instead was to act from what was deep in her womb, the very one that had grown the son that everyone had gathered to grieve that day.

She allowed that dark and fecund space inside her to give voice to something outside her. She channeled something so powerful it illuminated the darkness and broke through the bubble of stupor, like how a jet makes a boom when it breaks the sound barrier.

And once it found its way out into the light of day, it was witnessed in such a way that we will forever know in our bones the powerful source of transformational energy that is born from inside a woman's body.

We. Have. That. Power.

I had a wild — and awful — experience not too long ago that helped me tap into something like this. Something I didn't know I had in me.

My husband had gone in for day surgery at a local hospital for some minor injury to his shoulder. Earlier that morning, I had gotten a tattoo on the inside of my right wrist, and it was still wrapped in saran wrap, which looked like I was wearing a see-through Wonder Woman cuff.

The tattoo I'd gotten symbolized the union of the divine feminine with the divine masculine, with the line dividing them meant to be a depiction of King Arthur's sword when he swore to protect and serve them both. It's the symbol found on the well cover in Glastonbury, England.

Something in me said yes when I got that tattoo. I felt initiated — or marked — like I was part of something bigger than myself, and my devotion to it was now official.

So, there I was, sitting in the waiting room with my cellophane Wonder Woman cuff, minding my own business, when I became aware of this white guy wearing a baseball hat yelling into his phone on the other side of this relatively small waiting area.

He continues to yell into his phone and then starts to pace back and forth in front of this older woman and me.

He's standing, we are seated.
He's yelling, we are silent.
He's angry, we are uncomfortable.

The older woman looks at me and shakes her head.
Something in my body started to sour and then twitch, as I became aware how much he seemed to be enjoying not only his show of force that he was putting on for the two women in the room, but also the verbal assault he was unleashing at the poor woman on the other end of the phone.

Finally, after fifteen minutes of listening to him berate, lambaste, and verbally abuse this woman on the phone — presumably over some car insurance misunderstanding — I got fed up.

I stood up, not knowing what I would do next.

I am a very tall woman with a Wonder Woman cuff, and it was immediately clear he was shorter—and now that I was looking at him, I was pretty sure he was bald under that baseball cap, so my headful of wild curls was going to be a trigger for him as well.

He took notice of me but continued to rant as two elderly black women entered the waiting area, one with a walker, the other with an oxygen tank.

He now had a captive audience of four women, and it seemed to fuel him somehow.

I decided to do something. Slumping my shoulders in a now-familiar tall-girl slouch, I approached the man from the side slowly, seeing that he was at least 15 years my junior, and said: *"Excuse me, sir? Would you mind please taking your call outside?"* To which his response was:

SIT THE FUCK DOWN! JUST SIT THE FUCK DOWN!

Stunned, I backed away from him, not sure what to do, but super clear on what I wasn't going to do: There was no way in hell I was going to sit down.

This is where it got wild.
Or rather, I got wild.

I stood up tall, with my legs hip-distance apart and started to rub my belly with both hands, just like I did when I was pregnant with my boys.

My brain was freaking out, and I didn't know quite what to make of my decision, grasping at strategies that would explain why I was doing what I was doing…*Oh, I see…yeah, that's smart…if he thinks you're pregnant, he won't hurt you or make a scene….yeah, good idea!*

So now I was a tall, fifty-year-old woman with a Wonder Woman cuff pretending to be pregnant?

Nothing was making sense. And then the moaning started...or was it more like humming?

Holy shit, I think I was keening. Do you remember we talked about this?

I was taking long, slow inhales, and then letting them out in long, slow moans, which might have been growls. And as if this wasn't bad enough, my hands had stopped rubbing and I had joined my thumbs and pointer fingers together to form an inverted triangle.

Which, you guessed it, is the symbol of the feminine.

Meanwhile, short white guy in the baseball hat was not terribly happy with my choices. I guess they were threatening.

He hung up the phone and stormed over to me, again yelling, THERE, ARE YOU HAPPY NOW? NOW SIT THE FUCK DOWN.

I took one of my hands off my not-pregnant belly and pointed at him, saying, "You DO NOT get to tell me what to do. STAND DOWN, sir."

And then you know what I did? I snapped in his general direction and said:

BE GONE.

The doors of the waiting room flew open at that moment, and a nurse called him back into the post-op area because his wife was apparently ready to be discharged.

He went, and I sat down hard, rattled.

I felt like I had just tapped into something within me that had long since been forgotten — or buried or denied:

The power that lives in my body.

This angry white dude had found me threatening (or so I later learned from the hospital security guard), and at the time I wrote it off because of my height — and his pathetic attempt to defend himself. But maybe he had a point.

Maybe there was power in me that woke up that day, and he could sense it.

Maybe something in him was waking up as a result of something in me waking up — his fear of feminine power and his complete and utter inability to deal with it.

What I know for sure:

✓ Being of service and making an impact in the world is inextricably connected to women's ability to plug into something greater than themselves, be it a community, a mission, or a relationship with the divine. Like working the soil of a garden to coax life to grow, it takes not only presence, but regular care and feeding to ensure the soil stays well-nourished and protected from the elements, whether man-made or natural. This does not happen overnight and is not a one-time event, but it takes commitment to prioritize that relationship and move it from "someday" and "nice to have" to "essential" and "mission-critical."

✓ Women connect to service when they play at the intersection of deep heartbreak and righteous rage. Sadly, we don't allow ourselves much time or space to follow these to a source of inspired action because we are often quick to write off these feelings as *wallowing* or *not being productive*. We tell ourselves — and each other — we need to *get over it* and *move on*, instead of recognizing that we have tapped into the wellspring of truth that lives deep in the earth of who we are.

✓ Being of service and creating space for change generally means that things will be disrupted — it's how we move beyond that status quo. Disruption is often unplanned and is certainly inconvenient, which asks us to increase our capacity for discomfort, disappointment, and conflict. The natural world can offer an organic alternative to our man-made one. Think of how our shorelines are constantly changing, and how water will find a way forward, even if it's through a town. Think of volcanic eruptions and forest fires, and how lives adapt in response to them. Nature can feel violent, but at the end of the day, our earth is *for* life, not against it.

What helps:

✓ It might feel counter-intuitive, but spend some time with this question: *What is my heartbreak?* Take it for a walk in the woods, put pen to paper, bring it to the family dinner table and hold space for it. See if you can reframe that concept — for yourself and then others — to move from being *depressing* or a *downer*, to a source of life-giving inspiration to serve.

✓ Make a list of women who have inspired you — people you know personally, famous women, even fictional characters from books or movies. Get specific. What is it about these women that you admire? What traits do they have? How do they show up in the world? Why do they matter? Watch for *who* they are to eventually connect with *how* they use themselves to be of service.

✓ Be a giver — with your *physical* courageous presence and *literal* voice, not just your digital one on social media or your financial contribution. Get your feet on the ground, get your hands dirty, and awaken the senses in your body beyond your brain. Don't wait to be invited and don't insist on being seen or acknowledged. Let it be old-school.

Resources for now or later:

✓ *Whispering to the World* Angela Maier's story at Business Innovation Factory Summit (BIF9)
✓ *When Women Were Birds* by Terry Tempest Williams
✓ *Mother's Day Proclamation* by Julie Ward Howe (Google it...)

+ *Hidden Figures*, the movie

11

"What becomes clear, when we look to the past with an eye to the future, is that the discouragement of women's anger—via silencing, erasure, and repression—stems from the correct understanding of those in power that in the fury of women lies the power to change the world."
—Rebecca Traister—

Feminine C4

In case you're wondering if it's just you, it's not. Anger is the #1 topic women talk about with me. Hell, anger is the #1 topic *I* talk about with me. It's just...here.

Look no further than the proliferation of women's marches, protests, movements like #metoo and #times up, and other calls to action, and you'll see how not alone we are, woman.

In her book *Good and Mad: The Revolutionary Power of Women's Anger*, Rebecca Traister explores our complex history with women's anger and highlights the different experiences we have had as a result.

My most recent thought about it is this: If we don't heal our *internal* relationship with anger as women, we're in for many long dark nights of the soul. (There's a reason heart disease is the number one killer of women...)

Moreover, if we don't make space in our society for women to express their anger *externally*, we're in for a long slow road to change in this world.

Like it or not, our anger is here.

There was a time in my life, where if you had asked me what my thoughts were on change, I would have said *destruction*. That was the energy of my thirties, moving like a big wave onto the shores of my forties.

Needless to say, I felt some shame around that.

I once had a fight with my son on the way to school. It was one of those moments that leave both people fuming with tense jaws, bitten tongues, and cold steely eyes staring straight out the windshield of the car. It was awful. But this isn't about my relationship with my son. It's bigger than that.

It's about what happens when a woman expresses her anger.

Building up to that moment in the car, my husband and I had been jumping through the hoops of refinancing our house. It was a total shit show, and I won't go into the details of exactly why that was. Let's just say I was feeling invisible, undervalued, unheard, and shamed as a result — by the banker, not my husband, thankfully.

I started to hear those common phrases play in my head — *move on, get over it already, suck it up, don't be so dramatic* — and I remembered the irritation from all the other times I'd felt defensive and shame around what amounted to righteous anger.

I was just fucking angry.

Clearly, all this was stewing and churning in me as I got into the car and drove my son to school that awful morning. I started to notice and feel every irritant more deeply.

I got frustrated by the driver who didn't seem to get how to insert a car into traffic by just creeping the nose out little by little and giving the friendly "Mind if I cut in?" wave. I blared my horn when a driver ran a red light and almost slammed into my car.

My son, age fourteen at that time, commented on my driving. I got defensive. I got angry. And then I shut the fuck up because isn't that what we're trained to do as women when we get angry? Like Elsa in the movie *Frozen*, we are taught to *conceal, don't feel... don't let them know!*

We are taught to fear our anger because it could do damage, wreak havoc, lay waste.

But in my silent front seat stewing, I started to think about why I felt the need to clam up. Beyond the circumstances of my week or the particulars of the conversation with my son, I started to see the arc of our culture's beliefs about women and anger.

I sensed there was something of import to convey about a woman's experience in a world that is governed by white men, a club to which my son belongs whether he is aware of it or not.

It's not okay for a woman to express anger in our society, and I aim to change that.

I explained to him that as a woman, I have been shamed, shut down, and silenced my entire life any time I have attempted to express my anger. I stated this quite plainly and then added that this is not okay — and especially hurts when it comes from family, specifically someone I grew inside my body.

That was the beginning of a long conversation with myself about this. I started to think about the specific ways we systematically train anger to go underground in women, pummeling it down with a heavy wooden mallet in a never-ending game of *Whack-a-Mole*.

Here's the series of escalating steps that formed inside my head (maybe you'll recognize this pattern):

We tell a woman expressing her anger that she is *overreacting, being too sensitive, making a big deal out of nothing*. Somewhere in there, we suggest she *calm down, relax,* and be more *patient, compassionate, grateful*. (I believe we used to call women *hysterical* and take out their uteruses...)

If that doesn't work, we patronize the woman, patting her on the head, suggesting she is *all worked up,* has a *bee in her bonnet,* or her *panties are in a bunch,* using terms like *humoring, tolerating,* and *allowing* her to vent, rant, or blow off some steam.

If that doesn't work, we resort to shaming, suggesting (or outright saying) women are *stupid, uninformed, hormonal,* or *not capable* of understanding something complex.

If that doesn't work, we try name-calling and labeling women as a means to vilify, ostracize, and further humiliate them: *bitch, angry feminist, hag, shrew, cunt, dyke, witch, man-hater*.

If that doesn't work, we make women *invisible, disassociating or distancing* ourselves from them, physically or mentally *shutting* them down and *cutting* them off.

Dancing with anger is complex.

So yeah, you can see why women hesitate to express anger or are quick to shut it down in others.

Once, when I was visiting my sister, she pulled me aside and gave me something. She said she saw it and it *immediately* thought of me. She was clearly very excited about it, giving her eyes that special glimmer of anticipation.

She grinned and handed over a white bumper sticker that had written on it in plain black text:

Fuck Shit Up.
I loved it. And then I didn't.

I loved that she thought of me when she saw that. I loved the rebellious nature of it, envisioning myself as part of a merry band of misfits poised to spark a revolution. I loved how it didn't mess around, spelling out the directive in black and white like a permission slip to do what I was so very hungry to do.

Seeing that bumper sticker in my hand that day, I thought back to the first time I had read the *Monkey Wrench Gang* by Edward Abby, a novel about a motley gang of eco-activists hell-bent on protecting the southwestern desert from further development.

Sure, it was a work of fiction, but I felt immediately drawn to their gang, feeling like I could hang with the likes of foul-mouthed Vietnam vet Hayduke, feminist saboteur Bonnie Abbzug, romantic wilderness guide Seldom Seen Smith, and the affable and ethical Doc Sarvis.

These characters were not sanctioned, appropriate, or reputable in the least. Far from it, they were a band of rangy misfits who were tired of waiting for change.

As their stories unfolded, I saw how each decided to break rank with convention, had gone rogue, and were taking bold action to upset and dismantle the machines that were destroying the lands they loved.

They were total badasses. And they laughed a lot. In my heart, I knew I was one of them.

But then came the shame.

Fuck Shit Up? Wasn't that kind of harsh? And illegal? Like a swarm of locusts, all those *shoulds* that came with being a woman felt like they descended on me…

Be nice.
Play by the rules.
Be kind.
Wait your turn.
Be nice.
Be patient.
Don't be mean.
Don't be rude.
Be patient.
Be nice.
Be kind.
Be productive.
Be a part of the solution.
Be helpful.
Be fucking nice.

Fuck Shit Up? Wasn't that too violent? Unnecessary roughness? Who did I think I was? I wasn't this ruffian living out of a Jeep in the desert, I was from the suburbs of New Jersey and had 2.5 kids and a mortgage. And a Master's degree I would be paying off monthly for another ten years. I wasn't part of any gang, monkey wrench or otherwise.

Sad to say, the locusts won that day. I smiled conspiratorially at my sister and then stuffed the bumper sticker in the bottom of my luggage. To be honest, part of me was afraid of it.

What would people say if they knew how much shit I wish we could fuck up?

What would people say if I was honest about my despair and overwhelm at how backwards and broken so many things feel in our world?

What would people think if they knew the degree of anger I had about the snail's pace of change on so many fronts — the environment, social justice, human rights, education, government — and how sometimes the only *solution* I can see is *destruction* so that we might get a chance to rebuild from scratch, rather than make micro changes to fundamentally broken systems?

First of all, my fifty-year-old self wants to know *who* the fuck those people are that are governing my every move?

But beyond that, I now know better. I hear versions of that same story echoed back to me from women I work with every day.

Like the woman who came to my office because she no longer wanted to expose herself to the toxic workplace she'd been working in for years. She loved her work, but the culture was just about killing her, and it was clear she'd reached her boiling point and wanted to quit her job — even if it meant wreaking havoc on her carefully laid plans for retirement.

"Please don't let me blow shit up," she said.

It was one of the first things this woman said to me when she came into my office that day — a stranger who would soon become my client. I smiled at her as she plopped down on my floor because I knew. And so did she, it seems, as her eyes met mine.

She was absolutely going to blow some shit up.

That's often how it goes with my clients — their deepest desires are hiding in plain sight, and they are hoping no one will notice. And also hoping they do.

I don't want everything to change at once.
I'm terrified you're going to tell me to quit my job (or leave my marriage...)

I don't want to freak them (or him, or me) out—they can't handle that (read: me) now.
I know change takes time and is hard work, so I need to be patient and smart about this.
I'm worried if I start, I won't be able to stop.
I want to crack this shit wide open.
I want to take it all apart and see what's there.

All of this? It's powerful energy for change. Hearing it lights me up like a Christmas tree. But just for the record? I don't *tell* my clients anything. I don't need to—they out themselves just beautifully.

There is a fundamental difference between anger and violence, but so often they are interpreted as synonymous, and our fear of one keeps us from expressing the other openly.

But increasingly, as more women are starting to connect their anger with their deep truth, desire to fight injustice, and commitment to be of service, they are doing some anger alchemy, harnessing its power in such a way that it fuels them, rather than continuing to participate in their own shame.

So then the question that *really* lives at the heart of my work with clients is not about *resisting* the urge to blow things up, but how best to *honor* it.

I got a clue of how this might look when I stumbled upon a 2010 TEDx Talk by Chameli Ardagh entitled *The Fierce Feminine*. She began this like:

"I am here to speak about the fierce feminine. I am here to speak about the angry feminine. I am here to call forth the 'I've had enough already' feminine."

She immediately had my attention.

She recounted the story she heard from her friend, a seasoned social justice advocate who was trying desperately to find a rational argument that would make the case for why it was important to end a war in which so many innocent children were being killed. But she couldn't, so she sat and fumed.

Days later, this same friend admitted to her: "You know what I really feel underneath all of that nice talk? I feel a TEAR-DOWN-THE-HOUSE-PULL-OUT-EYES-OUT full-blown rage..." And she added, as if she needed more justification, "We ARE, after all, talking about children...children suffering, children in pain..."

It's been called "righteous anger," that sort of anger that explodes like hot lava from our wombs and is deeply connected to the belly of our world and this planet. It is primal and comes out in a roar with spittle flying, making us feel and look feral and ferocious as women.

It's not pretty, it's messy.
It's not contained, it's wild.
It's not nice, it's true.
It's not logical, it's primal.
It's not convenient, it's essential.
It's not comfortable, it's catalytic.

And here's the part I'm eager to get to: It's not about me or you (being right, being better, getting our way, proving our point).

That's where we fall prey to our reductionist (and shameful, for women) thinking about the ego being behind this. That's where we pause, and often apologize, calling it a rant, and offer to get out the dustpan and clean up the mess we created with our words.

No, it's not about you or me. It's about us — our survival as a species on this planet, social justice, safety and equality, and ultimately love and connection.

It's about our hot lava of love colliding with the cool waters of the wellspring.

So that roar you feel some days? The one in your belly that churns and burns and will not subside no matter how many antacids you chew? It won't go away. It won't ever go away, and you know why?

Because that's the energy of the fierce feminine. It's the nature of the feminine to continually rise, ready or not. It's patient that way.

And it's in you. Deep in you. Resting right between your thighs in a bowl.

But where I once was in favor of destruction, I now have a slightly different take on it, thanks to the performance artist Amanda Palmer and the music video she made after the 2016 election to Pink Floyd's "Mother." I literally cannot watch it without crying.

As the music begins (*Mother, can I trust the President…?*), we see some governmental figures — white men and a few white women, all in suits — overseeing young children constructing a wall with bricks.

Then, as the music turns more hopeful (*Hush my baby, baby, don't you cry….*) you start to see people emerge from their hiding places — dancers moving fluidly and invisibly throughout the landscape, people of color, women, older people, some children. And one by one these people swoop in and remove a child from the wall-building crew.

Meanwhile, other members of the ninja-like dancer squad take out each of the governmental figures, but not in the way you might think… this is where it gets really cool.

Rather than fighting fire with fire or engaging in mortal combat, the dancers swoop in behind each of the figures, breathing into them as they release their weight onto the chest of each dancer's body and are gently lowered to the ground.

One even tucks a blanket around one of the most exhausted-looking leaders, as if suggesting that he has gotten us as far as he could, but now it's time for a nap.

No violence. No bloodshed. No elaborate trials.

Just firm and swift compassion.

This was when the word *"dismantle"* came into my vocabulary.

As in: I want to *dismantle* the patriarchy.

I love the kind firmness of that word, and how it acknowledges it will require a delicate hand and some grace, versus a sledgehammer.

What a novel concept of leadership.

I believe it's the *feminine face* of leadership.

What I know for sure:

✓ Women's anger consistently lurks just beneath the surface of a few telltale words like *disappointed, confused, disheartened, frustrated, sad, or annoyed* in my conversations with women, and it doesn't take much to unearth it. It is powerful to name this emotion, however foreign, uncomfortable, or taboo it feels, because it often points the conversation to its root cause(s) — injustice, inequity, abuse of power, unchecked greed, lack of accountability, or corruption. Women's anger is a placeholder for change.

✓ At first blush, anger can feel like we're out of control and dangerous, but when that energy intersects with love, service, or truth, it becomes catalytic. The freedom to express anger without consequence is a mark of privilege — one that has been granted almost exclusively to white men. While white women are starting to talk more publicly about their anger, it is important to be keenly aware of how familiar and weighty anger has been in the lives of women of color. Women's experience of anger is contextual and begins with our cultural narratives and histories — not our gender.

✓ Shame cannot live in the light of day, so as more women give unwavering and unapologetic voice to the source of our anger, we will heal what has been holding us back: fear and shame. Actively practicing the expression of anger in real, unpolished, raw ways will strengthen our resolve to use it as fuel for change, desensitize us to how it looks, and change the narrative about women being dangerous.

What helps:

✓ What are your stories about anger and women? Get in there and muck around in them a bit to know them more intimately and begin to sort out what's yours and what's something you might have picked up along the way. Get curious about what it is you *actually* believe, versus what you've been *told* to believe as a woman. For instance, are you *threatening, dangerous* or a *loose cannon?* Or are those just things you've been called? Mine for details and look for evidence.

✓ Tune your ears to the words mentioned above that are often "code" for women's anger, or even rage. When you hear those words, see them as an invitation to ask: *Really?* Are you *really* confused…disappointed…sad…? Listen to your body here, not your head. Do those words accurately describe the sensations in your body? Or is it more like *pissed off, fucking mad,* or *ready to go ballistic??* Go for accuracy, not conformity or convenience. Name what's true, even if it's just for you.

✓ Be a word nerd a bit. Differentiate *violence* from *anger* — flesh that one out on paper, look up the definitions, and see how they get conflated so easily. Likewise, spend time with the concept of *righteous rage* and learn how that term is increasingly attributed to women's anger intersecting with deep service. Practice validating yourself when you feel it, using the phrase *"Of course you do!"* to anoint that feeling instead of shame it.

Resources for now or later:

✓ Chameli Ardaugh's TEDx talk: *The Fierce Face of the Feminine*
✓ *Good and Mad: The Revolutionary Power of Women's Anger* by Rebecca Traister
✓ *A Woman's Fury Holds Lifetimes of Wisdom,* TED Talk by Tracee Ellis Ross

+ *Elder Millennial,* a Netflix comedy special by Iliza Shlesinger

12

*"One of my mantras is, 'Embrace what makes you unique, even if it makes others
uncomfortable.' I keep that with me in my back pocket.
Shoot, I keep it in my front pocket! I keep it in my hair."*
—Janelle Monae—

The Edge of Crazy

Have you ever heard the expression "crazy like a fox?" I looked it up one day after a client shared this with me:

"I'm seeing foxes everywhere...it's crazy", she said.

This was a client of mine who lived in the D.C. area, commenting on the number of times she had seen a fox literally cross her path in the past two weeks.

Like me, this client had recently turned fifty and was in the place of feeling like she was now ready to unleash herself—her voice and her power—more fully.

Many would look at this woman and say she had already done that. She had a thriving business she'd designed on her own terms. She had a large platform and was using it to affect positive and lasting change. She was doing her own inner work. She was being approached with book contracts.

And yet. Something more was happening, and we suspected the fox had something to do with it. She texted me back shortly after her session with this: *In ancient Chinese lore, the fox acquires the faculty to become human at the age of 50.*

No shit. Well, there it is.

There had been something for me recently about foxes because, like my client, they had been finding me, and I had been drawn to them.

A large red fox jauntily trotted down the middle of our dead-end street on a regular basis.

I had impulsively purchased a stuffed animal fox "for our son" and had taken to calling him Foxie and sleeping with him in the crux of my belly each night in our bed like I was pregnant with him.

I pulled over to the side of the road one night and started sobbing, inexplicably, when I spotted a red fox in the middle of a field, seeming to stare right into my soul when I was driving to a meeting.

If you look up the significance of the fox from one of my favorite sources, Ted Andrews' *Animal Speak*, you will soon learn that the fox is associated with feminine magic:

"Fox represents that the world is growing and shape-shifting itself into new patterns that will be beneficial. For those with a fox as a totem, meditating [on this] will be helpful with creation. It can reveal what is growing and shape-shifting (or needing it) within your own world."

And then this…

"Fox has a long history of magic and cunning associated with it. Because it is a creature of the night, it is often imbued with supernatural power. It is often most visible at the times of dawn and dusk, the 'Between Times' when the magical world and the world in which we live intersect."

Um, yeah. It seems women and foxes are reminders of how feminine magic finds us in transitional times — which can often make us feel like we're losing it.

These are the women that find me. And this is what they'll say almost immediately to me:

I think I'm crazy. Am I crazy?

And then they'll list all the reasons why they feel crazy, ending each with:

What the hell am I thinking!?
Who does this?
Who says shit like this?
What the fuck am I thinking?
I am fucking crazy to (want this, feel this, see this, act on this)?

These are the questions my clients ask me every day. I know the sensation of them in my bones from my own experience as a woman, so I can meet them right there, at the edge of the dark hole no one wants us to go into.

"Crazy," it seems, has long been associated with the mysteries of the feminine.

So we know she's found the source, and it's rocketing up through her roots when she starts using the word *crazy* and talks in hushed tones, looking around to see if anyone from her world happens to be overhearing our conversation.

Which makes me sad for us because what might it be like for more of us women if we could overhear these hushed and messy bits of honest experience?

And I get it because I am that woman, too, and I understand the degree of vulnerability she's feeling in that moment.

But look for her doing it because she's right there in front of you. It might take some practice and keen observation on your part because, by the time you notice her, she's most likely already moved beyond it.

She's stopped taking shit.
She's started calling bullshit — on herself and others.
She's said no.
She's said yes.
She's quit the job.
She's started the business.
She's left the marriage.
She's galvanized people to action.
She's blown the whistle.
She's told her story.
She's written the book.
She's organized the event.
She's started a movement.
She's run for office.
She's been invited to speak.
She's been promoted.
She's been envied, admired, and elevated.

What you see is what happens next—after she decides she's not, in fact, *crazy*, but is the *sanest* she's ever been.

What you see is the *result* of what she's created, which generally doesn't reveal the *process* through which she created it.

What you see is the end, not the crazy beginning or the messy middle.

It's not because she's not *willing* to tell you or talk about it — it actually has nothing to do with her. It's has *everything* to do with our values as a society, and what we can and can't deal with in our predominantly white Western culture.

We don't like to show our messy bits.

Think of our relationship to **feelings** — like grief, anger, joy, and vulnerability.

Think of our relationship to **productivity** — how we are obsessed with doing, feel the need to measure it, and micro-manage it.

Think of our relationship to **creativity** — how we trivialize it, mock it, dismiss it.

Think of our relationship to **diversity** — how we "tolerate" it, call it "political correctness," and "manage minorities" as though they are a problem to be fixed.

Think of our relationship to **transition** — how we detest ambiguity, discount rites of passage, and systematically ignore the psychological impact of change.

Think of our relationship to **service** — how we see it as nice to have, a token gift, or a way of assuaging guilt.

Think of our relationship to **time** — how our clocks and calendars dictate our actions, how we never have enough of it, and yet we always want more.

Think of our relationship to **pleasure** — how we see it as decadent, lazy, and selfish, and overtly shame those that make it a priority.

Think of our relationship to our **bodies** — how we train, drive, and fuel them like machines, and berate them when they don't behave as we wish or when they break from overuse.

Crazy? Not so much, when you consider where we have landed ourselves as a result of these institutionalized beliefs.

These things I've listed above? These are the messy bits. These are the places where I play with women, the foxes.

She shape-shifts her relationships with these messy bits as a means to create movement and ultimately, change.

She knows if she is to move forward on her own terms, she will need to reckon with these messy bits she's never been encouraged to look at directly.

And when she does — the coolest things happen, like magic:

She realizes that these messy bits (emotions, ambiguity, not knowing, sensing, the power that lives in our bodies) are her natural state.

She discovers (more aptly, she remembers) that she knows how to use these things.

She brings herself into right relationship with the very things she has been resisting and fighting most of her life. She sees herself as *right* and not *wrong.*

That is a complete game-changer for the women I know.

And that, my friend, is often the moment she'll start referring to herself as *a witch* — sometimes in a joking manner, and sometimes quite intentionally.

Something in her has plugged back into the motherboard of her power, and now that she's found it, she's not going to let it go any time soon.

To be quite clear, when a woman does this work, she feels weird, vulnerable, and yes, crazy. She's often giving herself permission to go rogue, to break rank with how she's been marching through her entire life to date—how she was trained, how she has been rewarded, what she's identified with—and is pushing all that aside to give voice to the truth in herself that can no longer be denied.

Which is why when you ask her how she is or what she's been doing, she might choose to respond with *fine* or *nothing much.*

She's not going to tell you she's a witch.

She feels *that* vulnerable. And she's still unsure if she can trust herself enough with this, let alone those that know or love her.

Because in those moments—the ones that you might not see or hear about— she's banking on *crazy* being smart and right for her.

She's embracing being crazy like a fox.

So now, in the year I turn 50, apparently a "human fox," I'm lifting the veil on this world I live in every day and showing you what happens behind the veil when no one is looking or listening.

Because like it or not, we're everywhere—foxes and witches—hiding in plain sight.

And I, for one, want more of us to be trotting jauntily up the center of our streets.

So next time you see one, ask her to tell you her *whole* story. And then tell her yours.

What I know for sure:

✓ *Crazy* is a powerful code word for women, and to understand that is to find the trailhead to desire, ingenuity, and freedom. If you listen to what comes next after this word is uttered — or better yet, watch how her (or your) eyes light up as she says it, it's possible to get a glimpse of what is trying to come out and play through a woman.

✓ This is the place where *selfish* and *greedy* start to make more frequent visits to a woman's mind, reminding her of all the reasons she can't have what she wants and offering her loads of resistance in the form of *Yeah, but...* (Yeah, but you can't make money doing that... Yeah, but you don't know what you're doing.... Yeah, but you'll piss people off if you do that...). Resistance also shows up in the form of a saboteur, that "voice of reason" in your head whose job it is to maintain the status quo, offering you heaping platters of shame or fear on which to feast. Expect this — it's natural.

✓ Play helps immensely in these moments because it gives us license to make shit up, get childlike, and not take ourselves so seriously. Getting outside the box of our familiar surroundings will support your desire coming to the surface more readily.

What helps:

✓ Watch more closely what happens when you or another woman says the word "crazy" out loud. Is it a question (*That's crazy, right?*) that is seeking validation? Is it a statement that is leaving the door open a crack, begging to be challenged (*That would be crazy...*)? Or is it an exclamation of unadulterated joy, poised to take action (*THIS IS CRAZY!*)?

Look for and learn all the different faces of crazy in your world and open up to crazy being a powerful marker of something *good to come*, instead of the cautionary voice of something bad to avoid.

✓ Entertain this question: *What would I do if I were crazy?* Let that response come directly from your heart and watch as it has no choice but to bypass your head.... because you *said* it was crazy, so you're not really taking it seriously, right? This is the shortcut to your deepest desires, and you are giving yourself free rein to play with the world of fantasy, *just for shits and grins*, and *if I could do anything I wanted...* This is the land of flirting, courting ideas, and entertaining possibilities — where the seeds of inspiration live. Get them.

✓ Move this conversation with yourself into the world of play. Head into the woods and get away from the cubicle. Pick up your pen or art supplies and put down your Excel spreadsheet. Draw your ideas in the sand and take a picture, and the tides will work their magic and seal it with a kiss. Clear off an entire wall in a room and start putting all your thoughts, ideas, and inspirations on colorful sticky notes. Get messy, get bigger, and get wilder.

Resources for now or later:

✓ *The Power of Vulnerability* TED Talk by Brené Brown
✓ *The Seven Sacred Rites of Menopause: The Spiritual Journey to the Wise Woman Years* by Kristi Meisenbach Boylan
✓ *Plan B: Further Thoughts on Faith* by Anne Lamott

+ *Relatable,* Netflix comedy special by Ellen DeGeneres

Movement

How Do I Do This ?

THIS IS

the space of moving into the unknown. And everything that comes with it. A wildness lives within this place, making you keenly aware that you have desired or agreed to something that is far from defined. Which means this is also the acreage of vulnerability.

Different is the name of the game here as you head out onto the open road and soon discover — or remember — that all who wander are not actually lost. They're seeking. And you realize you are part of that club now, feeling like a kindred spirit with all those who magically meet you on this path.

Curiosity and intuition crackle to life here as you beat the bushes, turn over rocks, and search for meaning and guidance in every possible nook and cranny. Instincts wake up and want to govern here, like a feral part of you that has only recently gotten out of its cage and has picked up a scent on the wind or mud.

Play, experimentation, and a spirit of adventure help to lighten the mood, causing everything to feel like one of those crazy-awesome road trips that you talk about for years afterward.

You are called to lean in hard to this place at a time when it feels like gale-force winds are kicking up out of nowhere, asking you to trust more deeply than you ever have before as fear, doubt, and insecurities try to catch you up.

This is a bold place where shit starts to get real, and you start to surprise yourself with unheard-of levels of courage and ingenuity. This is also the place where people start to take notice of you and meet you with their own shit — disguised as concern, envy, or curiosity — which can leave you feeling both distracted and judged.

So, it comes as no surprise that this is also the place where we might change our minds, decide it's too much (or we're too much) or not worth it, and are tempted to scale back our desires with elaborate negotiations or counteroffers to ourselves or the creative force that is driving us.

But here is what I do know for sure: Clarity, insight, and serendipity live on the open road of the unknown, and it takes wide-open eyes, a brave heart, and a curious mind to navigate that road.

And while fear and doubt may try to crash your party, you are the guest of honor who will strut like a badass when you feel the wind of movement in your hair.

13

"Scary, scary, scary. Everything is so damn scary."
—Elizabeth Gilbert—

Brave, Brave, Brave

"Is it normal to be shitting my pants?" she asks.

My clients spend what some might consider to be a disproportionate amount of their time talking about shit — being full of it, having it in their pants, saying fuck that shit — but to me, that's a beautiful sign that space is opening up — but it also means that fear rushes in.

Fear is welcome at my party.

Let me pause right here and share with you the most common misconception about brave women who make bold moves. They are often called fearless, which — ask any of them — is complete and utter bullshit. (See? More shit!)

Sister, please hear this if you hear nothing else I say in this book:

She. Is. Scared. Shitless.

I don't know what I would do without fear, personally or professionally. I'm not a masochist or anything — I don't enjoy feeling fear — but I *do* recognize its value in marking a journey, rather like those piles of rocks called cairns that dot the trails when above the tree line.

When I'm feeling fear, I can be assured I'm on the move—I'm stretching, growing, alive.

For instance, take the time I played hooky with my two sons for yet another life lesson on the rollercoaster.

My boys, then ages 8 and 12, hatched their plan of attack all week, measuring themselves to make sure my littlest would qualify for the "real" rides, printing out a map of the park, plotting out the best strategies to hit all the rides, and feverishly consulting YouTube videos and reading reviews of the park.

Friday morning, we packed up some sandwiches and piled into the car, feeling ready to tackle any challenge thrown our way.

The look on my eldest son's face when we walked into the park told me there was one thing we couldn't prepare for enough: FEAR.

And there it was — *Untamed* — the hat-hanger of a ride the park boasted about on its website and glossy brochure. It was all gleaming white steel, rising up to create a stark, cold, menacing profile against a blue sky. The three of us stared straight up at it, hearing the screams of terror raining down upon us from the eight brave souls who were being carried on their way up, straight up, to uncertain doom.

We watched, entranced, as the faces of those eight terrified people gradually came into view, then faced us directly as they plummeted back down to earth and whizzed by on their way to make a full loop.

When it passed us and there was a lull in the action, both of my sons looked at me. I'm fairly certain I was grinning manically, having whet the appetite of my Jersey genes with rollercoasters in my DNA, and realizing I had finally reached the point where *both* my kids were at the age where we could hit the big-league rides. In my mind, I was planning road trips to all the big parks I knew. My eldest—ever the strategist—turned to us and announced: "I think we're going to need some courage. Let's go get a slushy."

As much as we had planned for this trip, studied the rides, and rallied ourselves senseless, nothing could truly prepare us for the actual fear of getting in line for this ride.

Watching my sons sip their hideously red and neon green slushies, I was reminded of what I tell my clients every day:

You can't logically reason with fear.

It's just not possible to stand on safe ground and expect to understand what fear feels like in the moment. You'll just go nowhere fast and be trapped inside the confines of your mind, like a mosquito frozen in a chunk of amber.

As I looked at my kids doing their own dance with fear that day, it was as if fear was a sudden outburst of rain that made us run for cover to wait out the worst of it before venturing out again.

Fear is not something you *think*. It's something you *feel*.

So after my eldest son had gotten to the bottom of his slushy, we marched ourselves over to get in line.

"The hardest part is just getting in the line," I heard myself say to him.

What a crock of shit that was, and I knew it.

Just days before, I had received the manuscript of my first book back from my editor, having waited for its return to my wringing hands since sending it to her nearly three months earlier.

So conceivably, I had been standing in the fucking "*line*" since deciding to write that first book the previous summer (give or take ten years…), and it wasn't getting any easier. It was, in fact, getting harder. I wasn't feeling any *less* fear. I was actually feeling even *more* afraid. And why?

Shit was getting real, that's why.

But we stayed in line, moving up little by little, getting closer and closer to the pathetically small cage we would be strapped into with five other strangers.

We wanted to be that brave. We wanted to be *those* people who went on that ride and lived to tell the tale.

As we made it to the front of the line and we strapped ourselves in and pulled down on the heavy shoulder bars, I thought of how scared I was to do the final edits and release my first book in the world—my first time going public in a really big, *Untamed*-like way.

I thought of how vulnerable I felt and how grossly unprepared I was to deal with whatever might come my way. I didn't know what that might be, exactly, as I sat there strapped in that cage, but was pretty sure it would be bad.

So bad I could die. Or so it seemed.

And that moment, right there, is the worst part of the fear dance— the part where we come face to face with our worst fears. In my case, looking down the barrel at my manuscript all locked and loaded, it was this:

What if it sucks?
What if I've lost my mind and people find out?
What if no one likes it?
What if people do like it?
What if it only makes sense to me?
What if I'm too out there?
What if I got it all wrong?
What if I've just wasted all that time and money?
What if...?
What if...?
What if...?

And then we were moving, gliding around the final corner in front of the sympathetic and worried eyes of the line members we had once been. Allies who also said yes to the near-death experience. Fellow fear-feelers.

Our cage tilted back ninety degrees, and suddenly we were on our backs, looking straight up at the sky with only a glimpse of the rails appearing just over our toes.

I started screaming, chanting as I do at the top of my lungs, "Brave! Brave! Brave! Brave! Brave! Brave!" while my mute children soldiered on in silence.

I thought back to all those questions I hadn't been able to answer like, "So what's your book about?" and how my mouth had this habit of popping open with a look of confusion, a look of pain passing over my face, before I snapped my mouth shut like a Venus flytrap on the unsuspecting fingers of the curious.

Always a sign I am trying to *think* my way through fear and not actually feel it.

It's natural, fear, and ultimately doesn't get in the way of the ride happening.

After our first (of many) rides on *Untamed*, we strutted around, chests puffed out with pride, knowing we were one of the brave people—you know, the *Untamed* people. We even bought stickers with bear claw slashes on them to show that we were, in fact, the real deal.

That's become a trick of mine to get through those brave moments with a bit more panache. I remember to focus my sights on how the after-party will feel, like it did with my boys after our first ride.

The sweet release that ultimately comes from surrendering to gravity.

Even if you poop in your pants a little bit.

One of my favorite stories about normalizing fear and desensitizing ourselves to its presence comes from my experience in the corporate world.

I was once working with a senior executive who was charged with rallying people to deliver on a near-impossible deadline, in a tumultuous environment where any number of variables could swoop in and completely derail the train at a moment's notice.

But as he stood up there looking at us, he said something I will never forget.

"The way I see it," he said, "is it's probably best if we all get a pair of brown pants because in the likely event that we shit ourselves during this, at least it won't show as bad."

Crass? Absolutely. But also, brilliant, as the crowd that had gathered that day burst out laughing and snorting at the audacity of his comment, which, I might add, demonstrated his humanity and engendered a shit-ton of credibility that he was aware of the risks.

Laughter greases the skids for fear to slide on by a bit easier.

Laughter and fear simply cannot co-exist, so calling attention to the latter by leveraging the power of the former is a genius move if you ask me.

Then there was the senior leader who used to keep her daughter's Groovy Girl in her desk drawer, so when it all got to be too much, she could clutch the little doll in her hands and smooth its hair. She even admitted it being so bad one day she completely crawled under her desk Costanza-style with her doll, away from the prying eyes of her colleagues, until she could get her boots back on the solid ground.

No one is impervious to fear. And it can't be outsmarted, outrun, or voted off the island. Fear is like the clinging sock stuck in the sheets when you pull them from the dryer — you don't even know it's in there until you start sorting through the laundry.

But here's what else I've learned about dancing with fear — it's not about the floor dropping out from under you that's the scary part, it's the anticipation of it that's the worst bit to navigate.

It has you reckon with control — and not having any.

So, can you lead without control?

"I want to make a move, but I still can't see what's behind the curtain," she said.

There's that damn veil again—or the fog or the mist or a brick wall. The reality is that we can't see what we can't see sometimes, no matter how badly we want to, and that's scary.

We're scared to leap, take a risk, try something new, leave the safe harbor of the known, trust, be vulnerable.

We could fail.
We could hurt ourselves.
We could hurt others.
We could die.
We could end up back where we started.
We could end up worse than where we started.
We could be laughed at.
We could be thought selfish or delusional.
We could disappoint others.
We could waste valuable time and money.

All this is true, of course. That's the hard part: to hold those truths as possibilities.

What helps when we are faced with these moments is to do what most of us work hard not to do: turn toward and feel the fear.

If we were to go bungee jumping off a bridge in, I don't know, let's stay Australia, and we were standing there with industrial-strength rubber bands around our ankles, ready to jump off this bridge, can you imagine how ridiculous it would be to try and talk yourself out of feeling afraid?

It's fucking scary shit!
Of *course* you're afraid!

That's what I'd tell us both up on that bridge. And the same holds true for everyday living, too.

The week I moved into my fancy new office, I had a complete panic attack. I literally had heart palpitations, and this fear that had clearly been lurking somewhere in my body came up full force and had its way with me.

This fear told me I was stupid to make myself this vulnerable, that all my clients would up and quit, leaving me all dressed up in a pretty office with no one coming to my party. *Boo hoo*, I know. Poor me.

But I did something different in that moment, and I'll never forget the power that moved into my body as a result.

Rather than pummel myself with more logic and do the point/counter-point game with my fear, I turned toward it….and listened, as I never have before, with compassion.

I remember nodding my head as I let the fear in, listening to it, and agreeing with it, acknowledging that it was allowed to be there and was, in fact, right to make a visit.

As I felt this fear, my whole body relaxed, and I heard myself saying, "Of course, you do…." again and again… acknowledging that this move into my office was the first major financial investment I had ever made in my business, and by making that move, I had gone beyond what felt safe, comfortable, and known.

When I think of lighting the leader fire, I think of also igniting fear—both can burn, but both can also illuminate.

The key is to learn how to be a better handler of both — with love, respect, honor, and presence — so that they can light our way forward.

What I know for sure:

✓ *Brave* is often code language for an action a woman is considering that feels *bold, non-traditional,* or *unpopular.* Put another way, she's decided *brave* is her means to get to her desire, as in "I want _____, so I need to be brave." This is important as filling in that blank (the *actual* desire) increases awareness of what you're aiming toward — and therefore your likelihood of getting it — by shifting the energy and attention to the object or outcome and away from the barriers to it (fear, vulnerability, doubt...).

✓ Acknowledgment, validation, and laughter are powerful antidotes when it comes to the hard work and sweat that go into being brave. I think it's why I'm prone to repeatedly chanting that very word out loud in the moments I feel it — I am acknowledging and validating myself in those moments as well as making an ass of myself publicly, which is bound to make people laugh. There is something blessedly human about unabashedly acknowledging our fears publicly, and it can bring out the best in us humans, as we relate and salute each other for our pluck, moxie, and courage for facing it head-on.

✓ Being courageous is not the place to expect grace, order, or anything that would remotely fall in the category of "pretty" or "ladylike." It is the place of stinky, loud, and unsightly things like vomit, gas, poop, swearing, and sweat. It is not the time to expect best behavior, decorum, or even giving a shit. Think of a woman in labor with a baby or someone jumping out of a plane. Loud and messy. Most of us know this intellectually, but when we're actually in those moments and living them, we apologize profusely and act surprised or embarrassed.

What helps:

✓ Play the *What If…. Game* with yourself. Make a good, long, juicy pile of fears. It's counterintuitive, I know, because we are taught that being fearless is noble — as if it's a real thing (*which it isn't*). Bring what's living in the shadows of your fear, doubt, and overwhelm into the light of day and engage each directly by asking sincerely: *What IF* _____ *happened?* Play it out: *So what if it did? Then what would happen?* How would you handle that? What would you do?

✓ Create an alter ego that will be your imaginary friend, your badass wing-woman, or your guardian angel. Seriously, it helps. Think Wonder Woman, Shuri, or SheRa. Call in your Navy SEAL team of supporters and form an energetic posse of badasses that will mentally support you in this moment. Or better yet, look to your real-life people and enlist them to stand by and witness your being brave. Let them buoy you in your moment.

✓ Avoid looking at or otherwise engaging with people in the cheap seats — the only thing they'll be able to offer you is more fear in the form of concern, doubt, or judgment (see the *Woman of Intrigue* chapter for specifics on how to dance with this more). Instead, find solidarity with those who are also in the messy arena — you'll know because they are also sweaty, unkempt, and wild-looking, even as they seem to be having fun.

Resources for now or later:

✓ *Seven Necessary Sins for Women and Girls* by Mona Eltahawy
✓ *Daring Greatly* by Brené Brown
✓ *Everything Is Figureoutable* by Marie Forleo

+ *Wild* by Cheryl Strayed (book or movie)

14

"Where there is woman, there is magic."
—Ntozake Shange—

Another Realm

"It's mystical, but it's not a mystery," she said.

Yes. My thoughts exactly.

This was a client who had entered my office three months earlier, saying she needed to clearly see what was next for her so she could make a plan. She shared that if she could come up with a reason to quit her job that day, she wouldn't hesitate to do it — that's how much her job had depleted her, deadened her, and left her not even recognizing herself.

She then went on to say that she didn't want to make any rash decisions, be impulsive, or wallow in negativity. She said she'd been feeling this weight on her, like the walls were closing in, and the monotony of her routine was leaving her increasingly uninspired and feeling trapped, a sensation that had grown in intensity since having had a baby the previous year.

And then she paused and said something telling about who she truly was at her core and what was trying to take the wheel of her life:

"I have this strong feeling that what I need is hiding in plain sight."

This is what a woman says when she's ready to believe in what she can't yet fully understand.

This is the sound of a woman's power being activated.

This is what is said right before she does something or tries something that someone else might think is "crazy."

This is the sound of a woman believing in herself like she never has before.

I call it "working your magic."

Getting to that magic requires us to do a bit of reprogramming, I find. And I will add that it's not for the faint of heart because it might appear bat-shit crazy to people in the cheap seats.

Think of Harry Potter learning he was actually a wizard and being told he needed to be at platform 9 ¾ on a particular day in order to catch the Hogwarts Express with the rest of the first-year students.

When he first arrives at London's King's Cross Station, all he can see is what the rest of the "muggles" (non-magical people) can see: two signs, one for platform 9 and another for platform 10.

He doesn't yet know how to get to platform 9¾.

He's completely unsure of what to do next—all loaded up for his big adventure, and no place to go. Thankfully, he happens to overhear Mrs. Weasley as she gathers up her gaggle of kids to send off to Hogwarts.

She points to the brick wall between platforms 9 and 10 and tells him that he gets to platform 9 ¾ by racing headlong into the wall.

"Not to worry dear...now all you've got to do is walk straight at the wall between platforms nine and ten...best do it at a bit of a run if you're nervous."

Yeah. That kind of bat-shit crazy.

That's the sort of stuff we talk about in my office, which is why I remind my clients often to be mindful of Muggles and that it takes chops to believe that Platform 9 ¾ even *exists*, never mind the moxie and pluck it takes to intentionally run your cart full speed into a brick wall.

When a woman is done-enough, frustrated-enough, hungry-enough, or even curious-enough, it's amazing what she'll try.

"Can you tell me more about this witchy stuff?" she asked.

I stood in front of the audience of women that had gathered for my Unscripted evening and marveled privately at how far I had come since my days of 360 feedback tools, personality profile training, and curriculum development steeped in behavioral science.
If the twenty-something version of myself had been in that audience that night, hearing me say what I said, she would have rolled her eyes, but secretly she would have also leaned in, hungry for what I had to say about all that "stuff."

The woman who asked the question had been following my work for years and was earnest in her desire to hear my experience. Like me, she had a background in consulting and had spent most of her professional life leveraging her abundance of masculine energy to gain recognition and make a name for herself in a field dominated by men.

196

This woman knew I had spent the better part of the previous year immersing myself in a self-guided intensive journey into unearthing the witch inside me.

Reading *Witch* by Lisa Lister felt like an acupuncture needle had been inserted right into the block that had been keeping me from moving forward in a way that was *deeper*—a way that was instinctively *mine*, and not just "the way" I habitually reached for because it was readily available, convenient, and comfortable to wear.

This was when I first gave myself permission to not only believe but actually *access* the magic I had been dancing around most of my life without actually "knowing what I was doing."

It also helped me to uncouple the concept of being a witch from being Wiccan, something I had never really understood.

One is a relationship, the other is a religion.

One is a birth rite, the other is granted through initiation.

She described a witch as this:

"The witch is a woman fully in her power. She knows that in any given moment, she can be a hot mess, a woman of grace and beauty, angry and grief-struck, loved and pleasure-sated, tired and soft, or raw and vulnerable. She also knows that in some moments, she can be all of this at once. She is whole."

I knew embodying and tapping into this side of myself more deeply would make me a more whole leader.

So on that day when I got asked that question about the "witch stuff," I had a lot of thoughts to share, and I had finally found my words and the courage to share them publicly.

She knew I had done a ton of research and had gone deep into my studies and exploration about everything from lunar cycles and sabbats, to working with herbs, essential oils, and crystals, as well as casting spells and crafting personal rituals that helped me to sync myself to the rhythms of the natural world.

She was not questioning the fact that I was a witch.

She wanted to meet the witch inside her.

When she raised her hand and asked her question that night, I could see that she, too, was done waiting. Clearly, I wasn't the only one experiencing hunger pangs for this "witch stuff."

I was working with one such client years ago, playing with the idea of conjuring. As in physics, we were exploring ways to draw in and manifest that what she desired by bringing artifacts of it into the light of day to honor her intentions and support her taking action.

She decided she would create an altar, placing items that were sacred and symbolic on a small table in her home as a means to focus her desire — or at least be seen and therefore more real.

But then she paused, and you could hear the sinuous roots of her Catholic upbringing start to choke the life out of her idea, dousing more fear and then shame onto her plan when she considered that someone from her family might come over and see it.

"I'm afraid someone is going to yell WITCH! WITCH! WITCH!" she said.

She was joking, but we both knew she wasn't. This was real, this fear, and we honored it as such, talking about how she might shroud this practice in the mists, like the Isle of Avalon, just until she found her footing again.

Tapping into the ways of a witch is *that* scary for a woman. It's *that* heretical.

So, in response to this woman's earnest question that night, I offered the audience what I am most known for: stories that bring it to life as well as illustrations of what I — and my clients — have played with, tried to gain access to, and practiced for ourselves.

I shared what Jungian analyst Marion Woodman famously wrote about the feminine — that the only way to *understand* it is to *experience* it. And then I began to share my stories with the hope that something in them might ignite a woman's fire to play with it herself.

Personal stories are a prelude to practice— where magic really comes to life.

"What do you mean, I can just write down how I want this to happen...how do I know people would agree to that?" she asked.

I understood everything that was inside that question and how absurd that notion felt, like a *wildly* impractical exercise that might prove pointless and leave her even more disappointed if it didn't turn out as she desired.

I understood how she might feel like she was simply setting herself up to fail.

I understood that by not giving voice to what she truly desired, she was leaving that up for negotiation, essentially hoping that others would come to a conclusion that was *remotely* in the ballpark of something that felt good to her.

I also understood that this is one of the ways we mute ourselves as women because I've *been* that woman—pursing my lips and swallowing my desire before it ever gets a chance to live in the light of day, insisting that people would never go for it, that it's wishful thinking or was too good to come true.

I was asking her to believe in her power as a woman to conjure—to make magic—and I *know* what a tall order that can be for women.

I was asking her to believe that every word she spoke was a spell.

Which was a big ask, considering this woman was also a hard-core scientist, a Ph.D. trained to *only* believe in what she could see, understand, and measure. Period.

She could have looked at me, the barefooted artist with tattoos and rings on all her fingers, smelling faintly of patchouli, and written me off as crazy because we were so clearly different.

Words are my beat and my jam. They are my familiar tools and my homeland. They're also what I use to make meaning of my world—and I have been rewarded my entire life for my use of them—communicating, distilling, synthesizing, intellectualizing, and conceptualizing.

I think that's why I love words so much—they're like these little chariots that I can use to ride into the center of town, casting them about with love and reverence or drizzling them with spice and heat to fuel a fire that illuminates and burns away what no longer serves or disconnects us.

But this woman? *Data* was her jam, not words.

And the idea of working her magic with them was akin to asking her to go for a trail ride on unicorns with the Easter Bunny while hunting for jackalopes.

Or was it?

Because I watched as this woman—hell-bent on setting herself free while also providing for her daughter—dug in deep and pushed past her years of training in logic, chemical compounds, and muggle values to play in the land of unicorns, determined to catch herself a fucking jackalope.

She came back to my office the next week, having ditched the spreadsheet she had used earlier to map out her *"ideal"* transition and came back with an old-school poster board filled with red marker notations and dates circled multiple times.

She had conjured something, and we both knew it—felt it—even if there were still loads of unanswered questions and big gaps in the logistics of how it all might come to be.

She had given voice to her truest and deepest desire first and foremost, not factoring in any other variables that might muddy the waters, sour the sweetness, or tamp down the green shoots that were trying to break through her soil.

She had cast her spell with the power of her desire.

This set her—and her circumstances—in motion in ways she might never have imagined. She started not only to believe in herself more deeply, but she also started to share what she was learning with her daughter, an unexpected bonus of passing her legacy of courage down to the next in her chain of women.

All of this ultimately paid off for her with a job offer that felt deeply rewarding and fulfilling, offered higher compensation, and gave her the first summer off in her adult life to enjoy the fruits of her labor with her daughter.

But this is just *one* woman's freak experience, right? A coincidence? An anomaly? Maybe she got lucky. Do you hear how quickly our logical brains resist that notion of a woman possessing that much power? Did yours do it just now?

That's the patriarchy that's living in us. It's the water we have all been swimming in for thousands of years.

We are trained not to believe in our power as women—especially that way.

Like crabs in a bucket trying to crawl out, too often women can pull each other back down just when one of us has nearly escaped.

This is where vulnerability comes in. It's a muscle in need of strengthening and a relationship that is in need of some deep healing as well as a good rebranding.

Working magic requires feeling vulnerable.

I bought a used Jeep Wrangler recently. I've talked about driving a Jeep since before I had a license. It took me about thirty-five years, but a couple of summers ago, I finally made it happen.

There's something about this Jeep that is deliciously impractical and wildly middle-fingery. It has two doors, and yet I have a family of four with a dog. Winters in Maine are long and filled with snow, ice, and salt.

But when I drive it, something happens to me. It's not so much that I change—it's that I remember. When I plug in my seat belt and turn on that engine, I hear her growl, and a big grin comes over my face no matter what the weather. Did I mention it's red?

I am *me* in that Jeep, and when the roof comes off, so does my lid.

Which leaves me feeling vulnerable—to the elements (*Do those look like thunderheads to you?*), to strange men approaching me at intersections (*Hey lady, nice car, can you give me some money?*), and to judgments and even envy (*Aren't you too old for that? That's not very practical…*).

One of the greatest gifts of that Jeep, though, is my ability to connect directly with nature just by looking up. I see the moon, I feel the sun and wind, I can hear the crickets and spring peepers, I can even taste a bug every now and then.

There are many days I can be seen driving around town with one hand extended up, fingers spread wide, spinning at my wrist, twirling, twirling, twirling.

This is what conjuring looks like for me as I drive from here to there, and it's how I work my magic in concert with the divine, talking and twirling and casting out my deepest desires along with my biggest concerns—up, up, up to the sky, and out, out, out on the wind.

Women's hands, it seems, are often our very own magical wands.

Which is ironic, when you consider that it was a pair of damaged hands that finally brought Dr. Strange (remember him?) to the doorstep of the magical world.

It seems we might all have magic living in our hands, something I tell my eldest son when he places his hands gently on my back:

"You have magic in your hands."

It's as old as time. Consider the three witches who foretold the prophecy of Macbeth at the start of Shakespeare's play:

By the pricking of my thumbs, something wicked this way comes…

Maybe it was the idea of three women gathered around a cauldron in the middle of the night, chanting, conjuring, and harnessing their powers of intuition. That shit just didn't happen in the suburbs of New Jersey when I was growing up.

Or did it?

Either way, I remember reading that scene in my high school English class and sensing the immense power of those witches.

I liked how they used elements of nature — eye of newt and toe of frog, scale of dragon, and root of hemlock. I liked how they worked as one, someone plunking in the ingredients, another one stirring, whilst the third said the incantation aloud.

I liked how they weren't afraid of the dark. I liked how they referenced the moon and its eclipse. I liked how they used the word *enchanting* as a *verb*. Something in my awkward teenaged body wanted to get my hands on that verb.

There was some cool shit going down at the cauldron that night. That's probably why Willy used it as the opening scene of his play.

The power of witches working together gets people's attention.

Fast forward many, many years from that high school English class, and I find myself sitting a circle of women of my own making on a cold, gray winter evening.

This chatty and highly animated group of eight in my women's circle got *really* quiet, quite suddenly. They weren't just lost in thought, they seemed to be *without* words — and these women were always in possession of their words, so you could see them stunned by their loss.

I had just asked them this question:

So what *is* magic?

It was slow going at first, sitting with this thoughtful group of women that dark, cold, winter night. But then something happened.

Their hands started to talk for them.

Lacking words, one woman started doing things with her hands — without even realizing it — first wiggling all ten fingers, then pinching them together and drawing them outward from the center, before flicking them together, like she was seasoning a stew.

We paused, each looking down at our hands like we'd never seen them before.

It was as if they were capable of communicating outside the confines of our brains, and it was the most natural thing in the world.

All it had taken was a bit of frustration and an awkward silence to release it.

People say that I "work my magic" up on stage when I tell a story and always comment on how much I use my hands. When I dance, I hear people say that they love what I do with my hands.

I now see that my hands, together with my words, are my instruments to work magic, and that storytelling is my form of casting a spell, leading it outward into the world.

How does it look for other women? Ask them and see what they say. I'm curious. Many of us are finding our way back to this, and we are finding our words to describe it.

How do you describe the sensation of being wet without getting in the water?

"I have never felt more at home and myself, but it's like I'm in a different house now," she said.

This woman was describing how she felt in anticipation of returning to her work after giving birth to her first child and taking a maternity leave.

I had gifted her with a coaching session, and we had decided to use it to map out her strategy for her transition back to the office where she worked predominately with older men, many of whom had grown children now but had had the privilege of their wives being stay-at-home mothers to those kids when they were young.

She was naturally a bit torn. She seemed eager to return for the stimulation after having been home with her newborn, but she also was seeing the world very differently now.

She kept saying how she hadn't gotten it before, and I've heard this many, many times from women over the years — hell, I've been that woman over the years.

You can't really appreciate something until you experience it.

But when life circumstances intervene—be it a medical leave, parental leave, or job elimination—it often does have the sensation of transporting you to another realm. You experience something life-altering that radically changes your perspective on who you are and what matters most.

It can feel like magic.

Jill Bolte Taylor talked about this sensation in her TED Talk. She is a brain surgeon who had the unfortunate and ironic opportunity to experience what a stroke felt like firsthand. Up until this moment, she had only heard accounts of it from her patients and had studied it in her research and extensive education.

But she never had the experience in her own brain.

Until the day she did and was forever changed.

Her perspective was poignant as she told the story of toggling between the two hemispheres of her brain. While she was in the process of having a stroke, first one and then the other side of her brain would activate. One moment she was aware of her circumstances (she needed to call 9-1-1), and the next she was in awe of her experience (how her hand was a collection of molecules).

This is how it feels to work your magic.

Toggling between two different realms—the material one and the magical one.

If you're worried about doing it right, I'd remind you, just as Mrs. Weasley suggested: "Best to do it at a bit of a run if you're nervous!"

I will leave you with this, though: You can't do it wrong, so just do it. Try it. Make shit up. Feel your way. Play. Let your instincts guide you. Read up on it, but don't overthink it.

See yourself as the magical creature you are and assume *that degree* of responsibility for the care and feeding of the power that lives within you, woman. It's all yours.

What I know for sure:

✓ Gaining access to the magical realm might feel like it's breaking your mind. When you start to see something that you've never noticed before, it can feel like your wires are being short-circuited, challenging everything you've previously believed. Our brains will rail hard against our discoveries, telling us they are not real and have no value or substance—insisting that we choose between realms, and forgetting that both can exist *simultaneously*, and we can toggle back and forth.

✓ Every word is a spell, which means the words we choose *matter*. Like acupuncture needles unlocking the flow of electricity in our body, words need to be placed very specifically with a great deal of intention. The words my clients use to refer to themselves (*wackadoodle, stupid, not ready*), what they want (*I don't know, doesn't matter, anything better*), and how they feel about it (*I don't care, fine, all good*), help me to understand what we can change. Words are powerful tools if they are chosen with heart and intention.

✓ Magic lives within women's bodies, so it makes sense that activating our bodies is how we activate our magic. It might be as simple as circling our hips, dancing to a beat, humming a deep tone to vibrate our insides, or going for a walk by the water. Our power amplifies through movement and is the spark that ignites our flow of magic that we use to create—and to enlist others to follow us as a leader. Ever heard of magnetism?

What helps:

✓ Get a moon chart or start to chart your cycles—menstrual, sexual, productive, or creative. Track your behaviors, moods, and inclinations, as if you were a scientist observing an animal in the wild, making notes of what you're observing, feeling, and experiencing. Do this for three full months, and then notice if you see any patterns or connections. Play with plotting your learnings on a circle, rather than a line, and see how you move in cycles naturally, even as you live on a line moving from here to there.

✓ Play with creating some rituals for yourself or your family. Don't overthink it. Remind yourself that you're making shit up as you go but trust that you can't do it wrong. You'll know if it's right if it feels and looks good to you. Use what nature offers you for inspiration: honoring the full or new moon, gathering people for an outdoor bonfire for summer or winter solstice, or building fairy houses with your kids in the woods. Reclaim holidays like Valentine's Day and Mother's Day by writing love notes, leaving affirming messages under the windshield wipers of parked cars, and planting trees or bulbs.

✓ Awaken your senses through the use of essential oils, candlelight, flowers, fabric, and food that makes your body purr like a cat. Sleep naked or go skinny-dipping in a lake. Pack a linen napkin with your lunch to spread out like a tablecloth. Put on music that asks your hips to move as you do laundry or make dinner. Buy or make some soap to use in your bath or shower right before you go to bed. Connect more deeply with your woman's body, and you will meet the side of you that is wild, witchy, and naturally powerful.

Resources for now or later:

✓ *Witch: Unleashed, Untamed, Unapologetic* by Lisa Lister
✓ *Practical Magic* by Nikki Van Der Carr
✓ *Holy Wild: A Heathen Bible for the Untamed Woman* by Danielle Dulsky

+ *Discovery of Witches* by Deborah Harkness (book or series)

15

*"Don't shove me into your pigeonhole, where I don't fit, because I'm all over.
My tentacles are coming out of the pigeonhole in all directions."*
—Ursula Le Guin—

The Lone Nut

We were on our way home, and I could feel everyone's desire to just get back to the car after spending a long hot day at the fair.

It was ten o'clock at night and one of those perfect Maine summer evenings when the air was cooling off, but it still felt warm and smelled like happiness.

I was holding my husband's warm hand and walking behind my youngest son and the girl who had lived next door to him for his entire life, turning into a wonderful hybrid of best friend and slightly older sister. They were laughing, talking about nothing in particular, and goofing around in only the way that intimates can.

We were almost at the Jeep—so very close—and then I heard the music, and my head turned toward it.

I could feel the other three members of my group groan with dread because they knew what would come next.

Like a moth to a flame, I gently dropped my husband's hand and moved toward the music, knowing they'd follow behind me.

Isn't that what a leader does?
Let the music move you?

In this case, it led me (and them, consequently) to a large open-air tent where a bluegrass band was playing its heart out on stage.

A big grin washed over my face as the lights of the tent illuminated it. My smile grew wider and brighter as the music reached inside and extended a hand to my spirit, saying, *Dance with me, you sexy thing*!

How could I possibly not take its hand?

More audible groans by my side, with the addition of some eye rolls because they knew what would come next. They'd heard too many stories about my days before them and had witnessed too many of their own to know otherwise.

The deal was done the day I was born, it seems, for me to follow the music.

My mom loves to tell the story of me as a three-year-old girl in New Orleans, dropping her hand and leaving her side to go follow the music I heard in Preservation Hall. At first, she panicked, not knowing where I had gone, but then she saw me up by the front of the room dancing with the trombone as it slid up and back, clapping my hands, completely lost in the throes of the music, much to the crowd's delight.

I just couldn't help myself. Back then people used to call that *adorable*, even though for me it felt *essential*. Now, I know that sensation as *transcendent*, but that would have been too big of a vocabulary word for me back then.

I just didn't understand how you could hear that music — any music, really — and not let your body move you closer to it. It just felt.... cruel.

Later, I would go on to find my people at the shores of a lake in New Hampshire, dancing for hours with my friends, getting sweaty, laughing, and becoming hoarse from singing at the top of my lungs, before finally collapsing in a puppy pile with them late at night, completely happy and sated.

But that was summertime, when the living is easy. Not the *real* world, right?

The real reckoning came for me in the corporate world years later. That's when I first learned to dance to music with the constant soundtrack in my head of that *Sesame Street* song...*one of these is not like the other...*

But still, despite other's obvious discomfort, I was led by the music to dance.

It was incredibly painful — a thoroughly cringe-worthy situation.

In an effort to boost morale after a particularly rough second quarter, the officers of the company had decided to bring in a band called Motor Booty Affair to thank all the associates in the company for working really hard.

The intention was awesome and spot-on, but this Maine crowd was not the dancing lot, unless they had a lot of booze to loosen them up — or so I thought.

I'd heard this band play before and loved their 70s cover-band vibe and the way these guys unapologetically rocked it out wearing psychedelic clothes, tight sequined pants, platform shoes, and funky names like Captain Flim Flam. They were fucking awesome and pretty well-known for getting a crowd going.

Except this crowd? They were tired, and it was 10:30am on a Wednesday with no booze to be found.

So, when I arrived at that massive box of a communication center, ready to dance my ass off, my heart broke a little at the sight before me. The band was in full swing, strutting their stuff in their funky white-boy costumes, and cranking it out in the front of the room on a little platform stage, while the crowd formed a large awkward perimeter around the far walls of the space, some gamely moving slightly with that white man's overbite move Billy Crystal did so well in *When Harry Met Sally*.

I joined them, dutifully doing my part to uphold the company culture for what seemed like an eternity. And then came the moment when I could take it no more—that massive space in the center of the room seemed to just be begging for people to come dancing, and I couldn't resist its call.

Glancing quickly to my side, I grabbed the first person's hand I saw who also seemed to be fighting this urge to dance, and made eye contact with her.

Her name was Becky, and I will always be grateful to her for what she did next and that unspoken agreement that passed between us that day.

She did not drop my hand but instead courageously followed me out onto the dance floor and started dancing.

I'm not going to lie, in those first painfully self-conscious moments out there, with all those people watching, I felt like an ass, and I'm pretty sure Becky did, too, but damn it, we were dancing!

We gradually got into the music, and then into our bodies. Our dancing became less self-conscious and more contagious.

We were having fun, and it showed visibly to this crowd that was so desperately hungry for any non-Excel, fuck-the-ROI sort of fun.

And then it happened.

Someone else couldn't resist any longer and joined us…and then another, and another, and within ten minutes the floor was full and the perimeter was no longer visible.

Becky and I had broken the seal with the spectators in the cheap seats and filled the arena.

I will never forget that moment — or that feeling — for the rest of my days.

That was the moment I realized I could lead simply by dancing my heart out.

Which explained the moans and groans and eye-rolls I experienced that night at the carnival when I moved us all toward the big white tent and the music.

They knew what was coming, even before the disheartened bandleader spotted us and said, "You know, folks, if you feel like dancing, there's some space right here up front…."

I did my quick look-around and took stock. My husband would have been game, but his bum knee had gone out earlier that day. I knew the girl who lived next door was incredibly shy in public places, and I didn't want to ask her to be someone she's not — or to break her trust in the relationship we had formed.

That just left my youngest son — the one who was looking at me with dread, knowing he'd been selected as the weak impala by his lion-hearted mama.

I grabbed his hand, asking for him to trust me with that look in my eyes, just as I had by the side of the pool that day when I first asked him to jump into my arms.

He sighed knowingly because he loves me that much, and as we moved through that seated Maine crowd that night, filled with lingering puritanical values that only gave them permission to tap their fingers and toes in response the music, I heard myself say to him:

"You don't have to do anything but stand there — just be present and I'll do all the work. And I promise this will only take about five minutes, max...."

And it was true. Within five minutes of dancing like an ass around the maypole of my good sport of a son, I saw people getting up because they couldn't take it anymore.

We had broken the seal, much to the band's delight, I'm sure.

I'll also never forget the look on my son's face that night because I do believe he got it. He smiled wide as I looked at him on that crowded grass dance floor that night with pride and said, "We did this."

All it took was a public display of courage.

Derek Sivers talks about this very thing in his TED Talk entitled *How to Start a Moment*. It's perhaps the best seven minutes of "instructions" I would ever recommend for a leader.

And it happens, as some of the best lessons do, in the unlikeliest of places: an outdoor rock concert.

He shows how all movements begin with one *"lone nut"* having the courage to start doing something—anything, really—that has them stand out.

You know, publicly.

As he's talking, he shows this guy, at what I can only imagine to be a Phish concert somewhere in Colorado, standing up and dancing in the middle of this lawn where everyone else is just lounging on the grass, talking, eating, probably lighting up something.

But this guy—The Lone Nut—he just keeps dancing. And soon enough, someone pops up and joins him, and then there are two people dancing. And then three.

This is when he pauses and says something really, really important, so lean in close, my friend, because this is where it all happens.... He said to pay really close attention to your first few followers because this is *exactly* the moment a movement is started, and here's why:

The first few followers are what transform the Lone Nut into a leader:

Think about the "Me Too" movement, and how it all began with one brave woman telling her story.

Think of Obama spontaneously bursting into "Amazing Grace" at the funeral for the children of yet another school shooting, and how the crowd of grief-stricken and rage-filled mourners joined him.

Think of Rosa Parks deliberately choosing to sit down in the front of the bus because she'd had enough (and if this isn't the same story you've heard about her—check out Rebecca Traister's book *Good and Mad: The Revolutionary Power of Women's Anger*, and you'll appreciate how history has glossed over that bit with white-wash.)

I imagine this is exactly what Gandhi and so many other of our spiritual visionaries were talking about when they instructed us to simply "be the change you want to see in the world."

Leading is about embodying the change publicly—not just talking about the change.

It's what I aim to do every single time I take the stage at SheSpeaks and many other moments in my life, like the night at the carnival.

I aim to take up *large* amounts of public space with my presence and visibly demonstrate the change I wish to see in the world.

But it doesn't have to be a big, fat, hairy deal. You don't need a stage or a book or a political platform. You don't need a title, a business, or a life purpose.

In fact, as my friend Jessica Esch (check her out at *Say It Best*) has been demonstrating for as long as I've known her, sometimes all you need is a body. Years ago, she created a t-shirt that simply read:

This is how I change the world.

The idea is that whatever you were doing and saying while wearing that t-shirt (taking out the trash, putting your kid into the car seat, gardening, talking with a neighbor...), and however you were being while doing it (kind, open-minded, respectful, curious…) was how you were, in fact, *changing the world.*

Just by you being you in that moment.

It reminds me of a higher level of accountability. I drive a Jeep around town that has a wheel cover on the back that reads *Spread Good Vibes* — no more flipping the bird or being an asshole driving that car.

My point is this:

You don't need to have experience or formal training in it, although sometimes you do.

You don't need to get credit for it or paid for it, although sometimes you do.

You don't need to be ready for it or comfortable with it, although sometimes you are.

You don't need to anticipate it or organize it in advance, although sometimes you do.

People don't need to be expecting it, or ready for it, although sometimes they are.

People don't need to understand it or agree with it, although sometimes they do.

People don't need to acknowledge it or appreciate you, although sometimes they do.

People don't need to be good at it or comfortable with it, although sometimes they are.

As Mary Oliver writes about in her poem, "Wild Geese," all you have to do is let the soft animal of your body want what it wants.

With wild abandon. And someone—I guarantee—will join you.

Which is not to say it won't be scary at first—but it might not be as scary as you think.

One of my clients tested the outer limits of her comforts with this and in the process, she learned how she was using her stories about other people's reactions as an excuse to keep her from really going after what she wanted.

It began when I asked her a question that I ask a lot of my clients: "What's your superpower?"

I could hear her over the phone, deliberating, wondering if I could handle her truth. I could even hear her roll her eyes a bit, deciding: *fine, you asked for it, but you'll be sorry...*

"Apparently I can channel a woman's soul through her pussy," she said.

And then she laughed, and I could almost hear her shaking her head, not believing her own words all the way over the phone lines. She wanted me to laugh, too, I could tell.

But the thing was, I wasn't laughing. I wasn't buying the joke she was trying to sell me. I was standing rooted like a tree, guarding the fragile colt-like truth that just emerged from her mouth.

This woman was a mad-skilled artist, and we both knew it.

I knew her story. She had hired me because she was tired of hiding behind her day job, when she knew she was meant to finance her life through her art.

She knew she had been chosen. She knew she had said yes.

She also knew she had been playing small by making it seem like a joke.

I had seen her paintings. I had seen—and felt—the soul of the women she painted as they butterflied their legs in her studio and told the stories that lived in their bodies.

I felt the tears, the fear, the rage, the desire, the dryness, the wetness, the trauma, the healing…the power…coming through her paint with swirls and gold leaf and intricate designs. I could feel that woman's story. And how by telling it, she was not only healing herself, but healing us.

She didn't paint a woman's anatomy; she painted the portal to her power source. The one that lived inside her that she might not ever have seen—or had forgotten was there.

I knew this power she had as an artist scared the shit out of her. Of course it did. No one talks about this shit at dinner parties or when rolling up their mats after yoga.

This woman had a right to feel afraid. And she also wanted to get over it. But this woman was also cheeky and clever, and we both knew it.

She was a wiz at getting other people to hold her fears and doubts for her.

But there came a day soon after we spoke when she met her match in the most unlikely of places, in the most unlikely of ways. And clever as she was, she never even saw him coming.

She was out west one summer for a friend's wedding and was waiting in line to catch the chairlift to head up to the top of the mountain for the ceremony.

Right before this trip of hers, she had agreed to introduce herself as an *artist* at this wedding to *anyone* who asked, as an exercise to prepare her palette for where she was headed and try it on for size.

So, there she was in line, and she happened to get on the two-seater chairlift beside a middle-aged white guy with a bit of a paunch and a nice comb-over going. The way she described him, it felt like he might have had his pants hiked up a bit high and had one of those pocket protectors. And glasses.

You get the picture.

Now, my client, she's an ARTIST as we've established, so she's dressed in something free-spirited and colorful with matching streaks in her hair.

They start with the niceties of names, where each of them was from, and how they knew the betrothed. But no sooner had the lift bar come down than he asked her what she did for a living.

She sighed, then took a deep breath and made good on her promise, reciting what she'd rehearsed: "I'm an artist."

At which point, he asked the obvious next question...about what *kind* of art she made.

Here it was, that critical point: Would she downplay it and lie, or would she come clean and just put it out there?

Would she be the Lone Nut that stands out?

Happily, she chose the latter that day, and just let it rip, telling this seemingly meat-and-potatoes middle-aged insurance adjuster that she painted rather large paintings of women's vaginas as a means to facilitate their healing, remember who they are, and rewrite their stories from a place of power.

By the time she had finished, they had arrived at the top of the mountain. She was firmly convinced she'd traumatized the poor fellow on the ride up, but she also felt pleased that she had a good practice under her belt to report back next time we met.

What she didn't expect is what happened next.

After the ceremony, the man appeared once again, this time dragging with him a woman by her hand, saying, "This is the woman I was telling you about…this is the artist who paints women's vaginas for a living!"

And they both smiled at her, wide-eyed and interested in hearing more.

I will never forget the moment my client and I debriefed that experience, and how we recognized the degree to which we chronically underestimate others' capacity to handle what we are struggling to own in ourselves. We use them as foils for not disclosing our truest or fullest expression of ourselves — hiding behind the idea that "they will freak out…" or "he wouldn't be able to handle that…or me."

What's really called for is reckoning with how *we're* freaked out by who we are, or how we're choosing to show up.

But that guy on the mountain with the comb-over who my client had underestimated? He is my muse when I feel inclined to play small because I'm fairly certain "people can't handle me."

He is the one I think of when I'm tempted to come up with lame, bullshit, unfounded excuses for why it's not okay for me to want what I want or be who I am more publicly.

He is my inspiration that we are all a whole lot more capable of accepting each other than we give ourselves credit for.

So have at it, Lone Nut. Do your thing, extend a hand, and see what happens next.

What I know for sure:

✓ Creating change and leading from a deeply authentic place is often about taking your foot off the brake, rather than pressing down hard on the accelerator. That's the good news. It's not about changing who you are or becoming someone else (good luck with that…) but about allowing yourself to be more fully who you are. It sounds simple, but it takes chops because it immediately requires you to reckon with standing out as different or (gasp) being too much for people to handle.

✓ We will often use the fear of others *freaking out* as a convenient excuse not to be ourselves. It's tricky because we think we're being considerate, gracious, and respectful, but actually, we're not being honest. These are the moments when we water ourselves down and put ourselves into a box of "normal" or "expected," forgetting we're actually wild and unable to be contained. We're withholding the best and brightest parts of who we are—from ourselves, from those we love, and ultimately from the world.

✓ At the crux of this Lone Nut topic is really an invitation to move beyond *tolerating* our differences and move into *celebrating* and *harnessing* them. This is opening us all up to the energies found at overnight camp, art in the park, festivals, street performers, and road trips. This is where we get more curious and less threatened, more entertained and less offended. There are bounties of possibilities waiting to be expressed through us, which will bring color, vitality, and a richness of community into a world that has lost its luster and spirit of adventure.

What helps:

✓ Notice where you are holding yourself back from honoring your natural tendencies. Start where you feel drained or tightly managed. Once you can zoom in on these instances, you can look more closely at why that is—and if it's within your control. Is it your fear and insecurity or someone else's? Is it wrong, or is it just different? It about someone else not being able to accept you or is it *your* inability to accept you? If you don't know, get curious and ask, *"Says who?"* to hear whose voice it is.

✓ How well do you receive what comes naturally to you? When you get compliments for something that feels easy and fun to you, do you dismiss it as nothing or point out that anybody could have done it? Be on the lookout for these moments because this is where you are participating in making yourself invisible. Leaders are seen, not invisible.

✓ See your differences as your offering to the world stage. Begin by naming them. Tease them out behind your training of being coy or modest by calling them *superpowers* or *freak flags*. What were you born knowing how to do that others might struggle with—do you light up a room? Read people's emotions? Hear what's not being said? Organize chaos? Galvanize people to action? Put together a perfect outfit? Hold space for someone's grief? Write that good shit down, and then ask yourself how you can bring it more fully.

Resources for now or later:

✓ *I Am That Girl* by Alexis Jones
✓ *Yes, Please!* by Amy Poehler
✓ *Bossy Pants* by Tina Fey

+ *Part of Me*, a documentary concert film by Katy Perry

16

"Just keep swimming, just keep swimming,
what do we do, we just keep swimming!"
—Dory—

Proceed to the Route

I've always had a bit of a contentious relationship with Siri. I can't speak for what Alexa's like, nor do I want to find out, but I imagine her to be like Siri's slightly cooler younger sister.

The feminist in me struggles with this feeling I have, especially knowing I am writing a book about women leading, but the truth of it is: I don't like to be told what to do or how to get there.

I'd prefer to figure that shit out on my own, thank you very much.

Sometimes, when I need to be somewhere specific and have pulled up directions on my phone, I love nothing more than *deviating* from her suggested route because I actually live in the town and therefore know better than she does. Nobody's the boss of me, Siri.

She doesn't like when I do that, coming over the speakers of my Jeep with her steady, non-specific voice to tell me:

Proceed to the route.

No shit, Siri. As if I'm not already doing that.

What does that even mean? I'll tell you what it means (in Siri-speak):

"I have no fucking clue where you are or where you're headed, but I don't want you to panic or anything because I know you need me, so just keep moving, and eventually I'll find you."

Or something like that.

Inevitably in those moments, I roll my eyes because if I were really relying on her, how would that be *remotely* helpful? Wouldn't it be best to say, I dunno, *"We're lost...pull over and ask someone for directions..."*? Why does she feel the need to pretend you're not lost?

What's so wrong with being lost, anyway?

Don't get me wrong. I'm a big fan of technology, but sometimes I feel leashed by it, like my neighbor's dog, Lady. Seeing Lady emerge for her walk was like spotting a Yeti, and in the ten years that dog lived next door to me, I *never* saw her off a leash.

Except for that one glorious day when she slipped the collar and made a break for it.

It happened in the blink of an eye. One minute she was sitting there beside her owner, idly panting and waiting for her walk, and the next minute she had shirked her collar and was looking around wildly, suddenly overcome with the opportunities of freedom.

For a moment, she stood, frozen, looking up at the empty loop of leather swinging at the end of the leash from her owner's hand. What I would have given to read her thought bubble. And then?

She bolted, as if jolted into motion by this great surge of electricity.

While we watched, stunned, she zipped across our dead-end street and disappeared into the neighbor's backyard. Moments later, she came flying up another driveway, tongue hanging out the side of her mouth, and her four little legs a blur of motion. As she dashed by me, I swear I saw the whites of her eyes wide with delight.

Free at last, free at last! Good Lord almighty, Lady was free at last.

When I think about those moments the collar slips off, I'm aware of the pressure of the split-second choices we face in those first sweet moments of freedom.

Do we bolt and make the most of our freedom? Or do we wait for permission— for it to be okay?

Because I will tell you right now, if Lady had waited for permission, it would have never come. And something wise in her doggie heart knew it.

She seized her moment and didn't look back.

I like that part of me that insists on being wild—I believe in it. I trust it. And I do my best to honor it, even if Siri has other plans for me.

I suppose that's why I named my business SheChanges—I can always point to the brass plaque on the outside of my building and say, *"See? I mean business."*

What I'm really getting at here is permission to roam—maybe even stop, make a new plan altogether, or (gasp!) not have a plan at all. I will take a stand for this being an *incredibly* valuable and productive use of time.

I've noticed my arguments with Siri are getting louder, and I'm starting to think it's not really about her at all (ya think?), but it's my own hard-wiring starting to short-circuit, asking me to be my own navigator.

Whose permission do I need, exactly?

On a recent family road trip down the East Coast, it got a little ugly. The nature of this old-school road trip was to unplug a bit, show our boys how we used to do things in the 80s, and learn how to navigate with a good old-fashioned paper map.

We had done a similar trip out West in a rented VW Westfalia bus, and it had been an epic adventure all around.

But on this East Coast trip, after visiting friends in Raleigh, making stops at both my undergraduate (Rutgers) and graduate (American in D.C.) haunts, and spending time in the Outer Banks of North Carolina, we were all tired and ready for home.

My husband and I decided we were going to put on our rally caps and do the 16-hour drive in one fell swoop—from Raleigh to Portland.

All was going fine until we hit nasty traffic trying to make our way from New Jersey to New York, and Siri got involved.

She wanted me to go over the George Washington Bridge.

I knew better, of course, and wanted to go over the Tappan Zee Bridge.

My husband was holding Siri in the palm of his hand—ever the faithful man but tempted by her soothing voice.

I was in the driver's seat, though, and feeling every ounce of the New Jersey blood come rushing back into my body after having lived in New England for twenty-eight years. In fact, I realized in that moment that I was not only the *only woman* in the car that day, but I was also the *only* person who had *not* been born in Maine.

It might have been three against one (four, if you count Siri), but I figured I got a weighted vote because of that.

Do I trust my own instincts, or do I follow the directions I've been given?

So, what did I do? Neither, but I bought myself some time by pulling into a rest area on the New Jersey Turnpike to call a friend as my lifeline. She had lived in D.C., so I knew she'd feel my pain that day.

Clearly, I was still looking for validation outside myself.

We conferred, weighed the pros and cons of each bridge and decided — gah! — that Siri might know something we didn't know that day.

Siri 1, Instincts 0 (but who's counting?)

And sure enough, it was a dumbass move not to trust our mama-bear urban instincts, and I stewed on this in the extra hour it took us to get home. I made a promise to myself in the bumper-to-bumper traffic on the bridge that day, though:

Siri was officially on notice.

Because what I value more than anything these days is *getting my bearings* more than *getting directions*. I don't want to be told where to go, but it's helpful to have a sense of markers to orient myself in the big picture. This is exactly the work that I do with my clients.

No one really knows what's going to happen, and that's the truth. We like to pretend we're in the driver's seat of our lives knowing exactly where we're headed — I get how that's soothing — but if we're really honest with ourselves, a lot can happen on the way that we didn't plan.

Sometimes those things are horrible and hard, but many times they are these happy accidents throwing wonderful things in our path that cause us to take unexpected detours that turn out to be the most wonderful things.

In my case, I'm so *very* glad I never *actually* realized that dream of becoming a Dallas Cowboy cheerleader (it was all about the tall white boots, if you must know), an ad executive on Madison Avenue, or a prosecutor in Boston. But I wouldn't have believed you back then.

I hadn't hit the curves and bumps in my life just yet.

Try as we might, it's just not possible to see around corners, even in places like New York City, built as it is on a grid of straight lines — and definitely not in cities like Paris, which was laid out in expanding circles off a star.

Bearings are like intentions—they give us something to aim toward and keep us moving forward.

"How do I know which way to go if I can't see?" she asks.

Isn't that the question of the day? Like, *every* day. That is the top question I hear from women. Do you know why that is? It's because of *all the stuff* that lives inside that one question:

Fear of the unknown
Vulnerability
Self-consciousness
Insecurity
Overwhelm
Doubt
Disorientation
Analysis paralysis

There are many ways to come at this one question, and many of them I have already touched upon, like movement, creativity, change of scenery, trying something different — and I'll offer a few more as we go further in this book.

I have two visuals that I always hold in my mind when I sit with this question from clients — or feel the angst of this question in my own bones.

The first is an image of a plane landing on a runway at night in the fog — let's just say before computer-assisted technology was available for pilots.

I've never flown a plane, but I have been a passenger on many, many occasions and have gotten hints of that terror sensation of looking out the window as I feel the plan drop and drop and drop — my ears pop and I know we're almost there, but I can't see the ground, and I'm pretty sure the airport in say, Reykjavik, Iceland, is right by the water...like, *surrounded* by water.

I can feel the panic build...and my brain goes into over-drive with something like this:

Are we too low? Are we still way up high? Was that a light I saw? Is that a town? Are there mountains in Iceland? Oh, shit, there are volcanos! Why can't I see any lights? Shouldn't there be lights by now? How the fuck is the pilot going to land this plane? No wonder this flight was so cheap...

And then, in my mind's eye, I imagine something that the pilot might see trying to land a plane the size of a whale on a tiny little strip of asphalt on a dark, foggy night on an island that has both ice and volcanos.

Runway lights... blink, blink, blink, blink.

Like a woman in labor, reaching down between her legs and feeling the top of a head there, saying, "Holy shit there IS a person coming out of me!" after hours and hours of exhausting labor, I imagine the same must be true of the pilot seeing those runway lights appear out of nowhere.

You know, relatively speaking.

The other visual that comes to mind is from the movie *Brave*, where Merida, the fiery and spirited girl who decides to fight for her own hand in marriage, finds herself lured into the woods she's not supposed to go near.

A little blue flame-like thing is glowing, and she wants to go see what it is, so she approaches it. But when she gets near, it vanishes, and another one pops up a bit further up the path, leading her deeper and deeper into the dark woods, one blue flame at a time.

Apparently, these blue wisps—or "the will o' the wisps" as they're also known in Scottish folktales—are believed to lead you to discover your fate in ancient Celtic lore.

And blue, by the way, is the color of the throat chakra, which is all about expressing who we are, communicating, and using the power of our voice outwardly. So, there's that.

So on the dark — or foggy — nights of the soul, when a client wants to make a move but can't see what's waiting for her around the corner, that's often what we look for to orient her — the first of those lights (or the first of those wisps), and then the second, and then the third, and so on, until they are all laid out before her in the dark night, like a glow-in-dark flock of geese, its V-formation leading her home safely.

Maybe it's a sign when you need it most — someone responds to your email (finally!), you get the callback, you get the grant, someone makes a donation to your cause, or you get a card in the mail from someone thanking you for doing what you're doing. Maybe it's a wild dream that feels so real. Maybe it's a message from a bald eagle that keeps circling right over your house and then lands on your back lawn.

In my own experience, I've had many of these, but the largest of them, by far, was the whale.

When I was working on the first pass of the manuscript for this book, it felt like it was pouring into me through a coffee straw — a massive download of... *something*... that I was trying to siphon into my brain through this tiny, weeny opening.

I had made myself available to it finding me. I had said yes and showed up for it. I had asked a friend to borrow her house up the coast for three days. I had left my children and thanked my husband. And now I was staring at my laptop with a blank Word document wondering what I had done.

"How do you make a move when you can't see where to go?"

Siri wouldn't even have an answer to that one, except to say:

Proceed to the route.

I had no map to guide me. I had no agent knocking at my door with an idea. I didn't *have* to do anything, *really*. Except it felt like I did. It felt...*urging*, like this combination of longing and urgent. You know that feeling.

The whole time I was staring at that blinking cursor, though, I kept hearing this noise. At first, I wasn't aware of it, but then I kept hearing it—and it was loud, like a friggin' massive pressure release was being turned on in a rice cooker or something.

Curious, I shut my laptop and made my way down the tidal river to check it out—or at the very least, clear my head.

My friend's house is at the end of one of those long rocky "fingers" that jut into the Atlantic all along the coast of Maine. They are home to the tidal rivers that start as freshwater inland and gradually turn to saltwater as they extend out to the mouth of the river to join the open ocean.

As I walked down her lawn, I saw what appeared to be a submarine under the water, but I couldn't be sure. At one point there were submarines up this way, but this river wasn't the one that led anywhere in particular. I thought better of it, figuring it was probably the late afternoon light reflecting on the water.

I made my way out to the dock that extends way out into the water, and then I heard it again, that noise, this time closer. Like, dangerously close. So, I stared right at the water for what seemed like fifteen minutes, trying to figure out what was making that noise.

And then I saw it. A *big, fucking blowhole*, spraying water a good ten feet into the air.

A whale, it seems, was right at the end of my dock. Not a cute little whale, but a turn-your-head-left-and-right-to see-the-whole-thing kind of big.

You can bet I reached for Siri then and asked her what the fuck the significance of a whale was, and she told me this (because we're back on speaking terms):

"Whales are associated with compassion and solitude, and knowledge of both life and death. They are associated with unbridled creativity. The exaltation through the blowhole symbolizes the freeing of one's own creative energies."

My whale, it seems, was asking me to write.

Would you believe me if I told you it stayed there all night, blowing through its blowhole? And then left just moments before I did? You don't need to believe me. It was my whale.

I believe me.

I also believe my dog, Max. He's a good boy (as we've established), but he's also this furry Buddha that's living in our home, offering us lessons about life when we need them most.

I've always believed that's why Dog is God spelled backwards.

There was a point in my business not too long ago where I was wondering what was next for me. At the time, I'd been in business nearly 12 years, and I'd done a lot I was proud of. My business was profitable, I had a deep and loyal referral network all over the country, I'd written a book, and I'd run many retreats and storytelling events.

But now what? I wondered what else might be out there for me that I couldn't yet see? Was there really something more? Did I have the courage to change my course and try something radically new, or was I too scared to mess with the good thing I had going? I didn't know.

All I knew was that it was keeping me up at night. Wondering.

On one of those nights when I couldn't sleep, I found my way downstairs to our red room (it's literally red) and sat on the floor. Max, of course, good boy that he is, heard me getting up and came down to check on me.

But he did something different this time — and by *different*, I mean *weird*.

When he came through the kitchen, he paused just outside the doorway to our red room on this little landing and, like a furry little Thomas the Tank Engine on the wheelhouse at the station, spun himself around 180 degrees and started walking backwards across the tile of the mudroom.

When I looked up to greet him, I was confronted with a big dog anus moving closer and closer to my face. But that wasn't the unusual part of it (you might get this if you've ever had a black lab, as you see a lot of anus…)

Right before I looked up and saw Max moving toward me, I was asking myself this question:

How can I move when I can't see?

And then I see Max, moving forward, but also backward. He wasn't able to engage with anything *visually* until it entered his peripheral vision — at which point, he had essentially moved *beyond* it.

He was *moving* without really seeing *where* he was moving.

He just knew he was moving in the general direction of his bearing (that would be me), and trusted that if an errant shoe or backpack tripped him up along the way, he'd figure that shit out in when he came to it.

That helped me tremendously — Good boy, Max! — in that I didn't really need to make a decision as much as start to make some moves to change my scenery a bit, which I did.

In my world, I call this "entertaining" or "flirting" with something. It keeps it nice and light—fun, even.

But recently, one of my clients used a concept that made me salivate.

"I'm going to play with prototyping that. I'll know more if I try," she said.

She had me at play, but the whole prototype thing just elevated it up to an art form.

As I understand it, the idea of prototyping something is that it's an experiment to learn, or in many cases even *break* something by testing its limits. In this context, failure is a non-event and a matter of course because the intention is to gather as much information as possible.

It makes me appreciate the power of language to frame our experiences — and why words matter.

Playing is to creatives what prototyping is to analytical types. Same outcome, different words.

What this idea of prototyping does, though, is offer a more short-term focus on her actions. When my clients get overwhelmed or paralyzed by all the open space of the unknown between here or there, I will often encourage them to just look at next week or this month.

It helps to contain and give some soothing boundaries to what feels too wild—like putting a mustang into a bigger paddock but not letting it out of the farm just yet.

Bring in the horizon.

That's what I'll suggest in that moment, when I see her face squinting mightily, trying to see what's so far out ahead of her. It's also why I have such a strong reaction to those questions that ask us where we see ourselves in five years.

My prototyping client wasn't *committing* to anything prematurely, so her tired brain was cool with that. She wasn't making an *official* decision, and she wasn't going on the record or giving her notice.

She was just prototyping.

Feel how benign and non-threatening that word feels? So, whenever something feels too much or too wild for your brain to wrap itself around, come back to the idea of prototyping. And know it's the same thing, just a different language.
You know what we're really talking about here?

Wayfinding.

It seems that's not only *who* I am as a leader, but it's *how* I lead.

All I know is that when I get away from all the noise of the machine and start to truly and deeply listen to what's inside me, it all feels a lot more natural—and effortless.

I stop thinking and trying so hard.
I start feeling my way and playing more.
I stop pretending it is a game to be won.
I start seeing it as a grand experiment.

I stop following the rules and expectations of others.
I start learning my own operating system.
I stop measuring myself by traditional standards.
I start creating metrics of my own success.

In short, I make it personal. But why *not* make leadership personal?
We are people, after all.

Women get this—they know how to slip the collar and use their own instincts for guidance—they proceed via their own route.

What I know for sure:

✓ I swear the answers to most questions can be found somewhere on the open road, where there is space to be with your thoughts, get perspective, feel your way, and get inspired. *Different* is the name of the game when it comes to creating change, which means whatever you are seeking will most likely be found outside the confines of the beaten path you've been traveling on, or beyond the limits of what your brain knows. It's why it's called "the unknown."

✓ Faith walks are for the brave-hearted because there are no guarantees or AAA triptychs that will guide you. These are the moments you look for smallish and yet highly illuminating signs that will offer clues that you're on the right path. It's also the *you've GOT to be kidding me* signs that come at you rapid-fire and are almost laughable, like seeing a bald eagle five times in one day. The key is to stay open and alert.

✓ It's tempting to hang out in the space of "I don't know..." because honestly, it feels safer and more comfortable than the alternative some times. We are taught to wait and encouraged to be sure and ready before we make a move. But honestly, it's not as helpful as moving, especially for women. Movement helps us create, even if it's just getting a change of scenery, going for a walk, or changing the way we drive to work. Small and subtle works.

What helps:

✓ Create a playlist that helps ignite your spirit of adventure. You'll know you're finding the right tunes if your playlist is reminding you of a road trip, more free-spirited times, or your maverick side that's dying to go rogue. Go way back if you need to and don't worry if it doesn't make sense — your body will know. Pull it all together, roll down the windows or take the roof off, and literally go for a drive to see where it takes you.

✓ Imagine you are on an Easter Egg hunt or are playing the game Clue — as if your life depended upon it. This is an invitation to open your eyes, ears, heart, and spirit to receiving signs from the Universe that will help guide you along your path. If you don't believe in them, you won't see them, but I assure you they're all around you. Listen to songs that play repeatedly on the radio, read the bumper stickers on cars ahead of you, and see everything that comes into your awareness for today as an answer to your call for help. Collect them, and you'll see.

✓ Invest in a deck of tarot cards, but make sure they are designed with a woman in mind (my favorites are Doreen Virtue's *Goddess Guidance*, Meggan Watterson's *Divine Feminine*, or Fiona Morgan's *Daughters of the Moon*). Each deck comes with a small booklet that instructs how to do a simple reading and offers insight into each card, but it doesn't have to be a big hairy deal — my general practice is just to say, "Tell me what I need to hear," and then I put them all face down, shuffle them around with my hands, and select one. Then I read what it says in the book, and damn, if it doesn't help me.

Resources for now or later:

✓ *Crossing to Avalon* by Jean Shinoda Bolen
✓ *How to Do Nothing: Resisting the Attention Economy* by Jenny Odell
✓ *Do Less: A Revolutionary Approach to Time and Energy Management for Busy Moms* by Kate Northrup

+ *Tracks: One Woman's Journey Across 1,700 Miles of Australia's Outback* by Robyn Davidson

17

*"If I could leave one legacy, it would be for more female athletes to admit their
ambitions. Don't let anybody tell you you're wrong to have them."*
—Michaela Shiffrin—

Going Wolverine

A client once came to my office one day holding a picture of a little girl in a swimsuit, arms and legs spread wide like a starfish. Her face was scrunched up in a primal yell, and water was flying off of her in all directions from a sprinkler. The caption on the picture read:

Remember Her? Let's go get her.

My client, now in her late 50s, looked at me with tears in her eyes and said, "This."

She was remembering—and then grabbing on tight—to her favorite part of herself, and I could see that girl now in her wise woman face, beaming with delight. Happy to be caught.

Because the thing that I've come to love about that girl in us?

It's not in her nature to shrink or wait, and because of that, she's unforgettable, timeless, and enduring. The feminine—she continually rises, remember?

And each time she rises, it's like she brings another piece of ourselves to the surface, something we had long ago lost or buried, and extends it to us as an offering, saying, "Don't you want this?"

She might be gone, but she will never be denied. She's fucking tenacious like that.

As a girl, I gravitated to books with characters like Pippi Long-stocking, Ramona the Brave, and Anne of Green Gables.

They were spirited, free, and unencumbered.

They marched to the beat of their own drums.

Pippi kept her horse, Nelson, in the house and possessed uncanny amounts of strength for a girl her size.

Anne was wickedly smart and set her imagination free, giving beautiful names to the wonders of nature around her.

Ramona was just the right amount of wrong, which made getting into trouble an adventure, rather than causing any real harm.

When I think about who I am as a leader today, these girls are actually my inspiration. But they are all about age nine—how sad is that—and how telling of what we do to our girls?

At some point in my life, I turned on these girls as well, concluding they didn't look the part of a leader, I suppose, with all that red hair and pigtails sticking out, freckles and dirt and bangs cut by hand.

If I'm honest, I threw these girls I admired under the bus and never looked back.

Until the day I heard myself referring to who I was and how I did it as a *freak* or *freakish*. As in,

"I have this *freakish* ability…."

"I can *freak* people out if I'm not careful."
"You're gonna think I'm a *freak*, but…"

I thought of one of my favorite songs, "Super Freak" by Rick James, and how it gets me going on the dance floor.

Interestingly enough, all of this made me think of not just my imagination, but also my creative spirit and my ability to move my body.

It made me think of the artist in me, and how I'd also thrown *her* under the bus for years by mocking my art major or dismissing my artistic endeavors as *nothing, silly,* and *a joke* — abandoning an essential part of myself in my pursuit to be *professional* and *accomplished, serious* and *important.*

Then I realized—holy shit, I *am* that girl I threw under the bus.

What had I done? I had let her go. I tried to bury her alive. And I did my best to try and forget her. Even though she's really the only person I know how to be — honestly.

I see this same look — a little tearful, a little wistful — in the eyes of each and every woman I work with at some point in time. It's that moment when a woman realizes, just as I did.

That girl is *exactly* the wing woman she needs to get her where she wants to go.

"I forgot I used to yodel", she said.

And she paused, lost in her own thoughts as she remembered who she was before the world told her who she was supposed to be.

As a girl, she would go into the fields, meadows, and woods, exploring and communing. And at the end of the day, when it was time to head home, she would yodel to call the dogs home.

Looking at her now, I could see the yodeler in her. I could also see the layers of living that had kept the full wattage of her yodeling capacity inside.

In fact, my experience of this woman, who would later become one of my dearest friends, was that she was a powerhouse inside a skin-and-bones container that insisted her voice be even-keeled, well-modulated, and deliberately used to gently illuminate, rather than explosively ignite.

She was a journalist by trade and she loved her work, but I could tell she was itching to see if she could still do it—both yodel and to find her way home. It was clear just looking at her that she was sure as hell going to try. Even if people got freaked out by it.

Publicly and proudly honoring what comes naturally is how we ignite our leader fire.

Which, I'm not gonna lie, can be challenging in the face of all that training we've had as women.

Think about the messages we get on a daily basis that most of us have equated with work, productivity, leadership, strength, and success?

No pain, no gain.
What doesn't kill you makes you stronger.
Fight to the death.
There's no such thing as a free lunch.
Nothing worth having comes easy.
No short cuts.

Money doesn't grow on trees.
Leave it all on the track.
Hard work builds character.
It puts hair on your chest.
Ride it hard and put it away sweaty.
There's no substitute for hard work.
What comes easy won't last, what lasts won't come easy.
Sleep when you're dead.
Hard work never killed anyone.

Is it any wonder why doing something that feels natural or easy often feels like cheating? Too often, we discount, dismiss, or distract from our wins by saying they're due to luck, the team, or being in the right place at the right time.

And all of that *may* have come into play, but it's often not the *primary* reason for our success.

Sometimes a woman's natural abilities are the sole reason for her success.

But how often do you hear someone—a gold medalist, a CEO, a post-partum mother—say, "That was so much fucking fun, and so full of ease!"

Um, no. But wouldn't it be cool if we did?

Okay, so I'm lying to you here. My midwife still reminds me that my first words after actively pushing for six-and-a-half hours to get my firstborn son out were:

"I cannot fucking wait to do that again!"

I shit you not. And in the spirit of full disclosure, I also wrote my first book in twenty days. I have *never* admitted either of those publicly, and you know why? Because I felt ashamed. And when I tried, I got *Yeah Butted*, which took all the sweetness out of what I was feeling. So I stopped.

But here I am. Sharing this publicly — because I'm fucking tenacious like that. Pippi, Anne, and Ramona would be proud of me.

But I haven't always been that way. It's taken loads of practice.

"Why do you do that thing with your face?" my husband asked.

I had just finished a sprint triathlon, and he was waiting for me with our then-toddler-aged son.

I didn't need to ask what thing he was talking about. I knew damn well what he was talking about because my asshole coach in high school used to yell at me for doing it — wasting precious energy by scrunching up my face.

I had been *playing* the part of an athlete, rather than simply *being* one.

I felt the need to add drama and visible suffering to demonstrate the degree to which I was working that day. When in fact, the effort I was exerting was flowing quite naturally from me — in part because of all the training I had done to get ready for that day, but also because I was experiencing an inner confidence that comes from being naturally athletic and competitive.

Despite having felt really strong out there and completely in the zone, I had felt the need to put on a show for anyone who witnessed me that day — even myself.

So much so, I had missed a moment of pride and affirmation from my child as he held up a homemade poster that read *Go, Mommy, Go!* He had noticed me not noticing him.

I had broken his heart with my face.

Was I a bad mother because of this? No, I knew I was a good mom, and this would be one of many stings I would inadvertently inflict upon my child over the years, I was sure. It was the first of many coins I would toss into the resilience fund for my children.

But I'd missed the opportunity to show him how fun and effortless it can feel when someone is doing something they were built to do.

We're trained, conditioned, and rewarded to show we're working hard—even when it's coming naturally.

"Help, I need you," she wrote in a text.

I knew this woman well enough to know she didn't need my help. She was a total badass, and both of us knew it.

I had worked with this senior leader off and on for a number of years, watching her navigate ladders, dodge seniority, jump countless rungs on the corporate ladder, and get herself a seat at the table despite the odds and not having the officer title that typically earned it.

I had watched and celebrated her make bold moves inside her organization, hit walls (and ceilings), and then take a big leap into another organization, relocating her family halfway across the country in favor of an organization that did value her and her contributions.

This client of mine was not someone who generally texted me asking for help in between our sessions, so I texted her back, asking what was up.

She explained how her boss had just given his notice, and word on the street was that she was going to be named his replacement as VP.

And then she put one of those emoticons that had the terrified expression of gritting teeth.

Huh. This news wasn't a surprise to me, as she had been sniffing the possibility of this move for months. She had a solid relationship with this guy, her boss, who had always been a fierce champion of hers, often encouraging her to take bolder actions and rely on her instincts more as a leader.

She was born to command the ship. She knew it. They knew it. And here it was—her moment—happening.

She was poised for promotion to VP, a position she had been wanting and working toward all these years. And yet the emoticon I was getting from her that day was nervous terror.

So, I called her on it, asking her to check if her *actual* face resembled the *emoticon* face.

Her text came back quickly. Turns out she was smiling, ecstatic, over-the-moon happy. Not a grimace in sight.

She had unconsciously assumed someone else's face, not her own.

In that moment, she had forgotten who she was, losing sight of the fact that she was a total badass, had been dreaming about this for decades, preparing for it for years, and ready for it for months.

She, like me, had fallen prey to the role she *thought* she was supposed to play — the one of the nervous but eager and grateful-for-the-opportunity go-getter — as opposed to the way she was *naturally* feeling.

But then, she dropped the act, allowed herself to exhale, and thoroughly enjoyed her moment.

She gave herself permission for this not to be hard.

But it begs the question: How else might we use all that energy that we women have been expending in trying to prove ourselves to others?

What if all that energy we have been using to *play the game* could be used to improve not only our performance as leaders but also *enhance* our experience of it.

Imagine more women being present to their leadership as it was *actually* happening, as opposed to thinking about how they *should* look as it was happening.

What if we just decided to put down all that shit that's not ours and focus on ourselves more?

"I'm not going to eat the need anymore," she said.

This is a woman who had been doing this her whole life, and she was done trying to pull more blood from a stone. She knew better.

She had always been a fighter and had leaned heavily into that strength of hers when it came to extricating herself from a toxic marriage, fiercely protecting her kids, and creating a solid financial and emotional foundation for them and herself.

She had physically carved out a place for herself professionally that included a seat at a predominately male populated table by working lots of long, hard hours year after year and burning the candle at both ends to make it all work.

And then, just when she finally caught her breath and created that stable base, she found the strength to open her heart to love again and take the leash off of her ambition.

This was a woman, like many of us, who has a long and complicated history with time — waiting for it, never having enough of it, making the most of it, wanting more of it, managing it, measuring herself by it, selecting right from wrong, crushing it, bending it.

She was a time ninja, probably like you are.

She had mastered what she needed to, proven to herself and others she could do it, and now she was done with all that shit.

It was her time now, and she wanted more.

It is a bold act for a successful and accomplished woman to admit she wants more. Because often what comes her way are things that require her to get *busier* — challenging tasks, special projects, growth opportunities, committees, and initiatives.

That would benefit those who work with her and for her in an organization, as well as ultimately benefiting the shareholders she serves, but what about actually benefiting *her*?

By *doing* more is she also *receiving* more — recognition, compensation, awards, freedom, and prestige?

Women in the sports arenas are all over this these days.

Two-time Olympic Gold medalist and World Cup skier Michaela Shriffin talks openly and unapologetically about her desire for multiple gold medals and in doing so clearly states her intention to leave a legacy of ambition for female athletes coming up behind her.

When she came up one medal short of her stated goal in the 2018 Olympics, an interviewer had asked her if she thought she had been a bit too ambitious, maybe set her sights too high...

How often do we ask men if they're being too ambitious?

How often do we have "Empowering Men" conferences that generate hundreds of thousands of dollars in revenue for men to feel like they're enough? (*Side note: Can we please change those to POWER conferences, women?*)

How often are men told to be patient, grateful, or that they need to pick their battles?

How often are men told they are lucky, blessed, and should be grateful to have a seat at the table or an opportunity to leverage or showcase their leadership strengths?

Abby Wambach is a two-time Olympic Gold medalist and Women's World cup champion who helped put women's soccer on the map by being the highest scoring soccer player ever in the history of the sport — men or women.

She likens women at this time in history to the wolves that were reintroduced to Yellowstone National Park in 1995, in that they were once seen as threats to the ecosystem but turned out to be its salvation.

She popularized the term Wolfpack (Google #wolfpack) during that speech, using it as a rallying cry to unite women behind a unifying heartbeat and storm the valleys together — to be our salvation.

A good friend put her own spin on this years ago, giving me something I would later envision to be the fierce face of the feminine.

She calls it *"going all wolverine"* on something.

That was me the day I was trying to move another human being through my body and into this world.

I got naked in the birthing room and started moving around more, at one point agreeing to suspend myself from a trapeze contraption that my clever midwife rigged up for me.

I started making noises that I never imagined I could (or would) make — growling, snarling, deep guttural bone-rattling wails that felt like they could travel for miles across the air, land, and water of our coastal town on that cold November night.

That was me, giving both reins and full permission to my body to know what it knows, to do what it does, to guide me and my weary head and spirit out of this purgatory place.

That was me not giving a fuck about what people were saying, how I looked, what was happening (or not happening), or how they felt about it.

That was me no longer worrying about making progress, doing it right, making people uncomfortable, or dripping, leaking, or spewing bodily fluids on the linens or people's shoes. Or faces.

That was me going all wolverine. Going feral. In service of new life being born.

And it worked. My very large son finally came into this world with a look of complete dismay on his face, in what I can only describe as a "What the FUCK was THAT about!?" expression in his eyes.

But he was out. Regardless of his expression and what he thought. He was out. And here. You're welcome.

And that, my friend, is often what I see every day with the women I get the honor of witnessing. Not necessarily mothering, but women who actively possess *that* level of *wildness* within themselves.

That distinctly feminine form of rocket fuel we carry in our bodies—that doesn't need a baby or even a uterus to come out and play.

Our bodies are built with those moments in mind. I believe the term for it is "creation" — as in life.

Maybe that's why wolves, women, and witches are as seen as threatening — as dangerous.
We are wild.
We create ruckuses.
We go all wolverine.
We are forces of nature.
We are capable of dismantling.
We are capable of creation.
We work alone and we work as a pack.

And all we have ever needed are our bodies and each other.

That's why I believe in women now more than ever with all my big, red, fiery heart.

A woman full of herself is a woman on a mission. Naturally.

Be that woman. Get full of yourself and watch how natural and full of ease it all starts to feel.

Do that, and people will follow your lead. Because wouldn't you?

What I know for sure:

✓ There is much discussion among women about the need to "play big," which I find most concerning because it sets us up to aspire to be like something "out there," rather than embody what is already "in here." Look at any nine-year-old girl, and you will see that we are *born big* but are taught to play small. It's a nuance in our language, but it's significant.

✓ At the heart of this conversation about going wolverine is giving ourselves full permission and a wider berth to let our ambitions intersect with our natural abilities. It's about letting it come naturally, having it be easy, and allowing it to be fun. It's about concentrating our energies and focusing on our greatest strengths, rather than trying to be well-rounded — investing in who we *actually* are, rather than chasing the illusion of what we're supposed to be.

✓ There is a public component of going wolverine that is critical to our success as leaders. It's important to be seen and recognized, for sure, but the key is for us to stand in that public spotlight and receive that acknowledgment if we are to inspire others to follow our lead. This is where humility and ambition can come into conflict with each other unnecessarily, insisting we choose one over the other, which can be our fatal flaw as women. The invitation is to hold the truth of our humility while also holding the truth of our ambition, knowing there is power, not conflict, inherent in that act.

What helps:

✓ Dig through your photo albums and see if you can find a picture of yourself as a little girl (age 5-9) that depicts your true, unadulterated self — the one who made no apologies for who she was and didn't bother to hide it from others. You'll know it when you see it—or rather, you'll *feel* it when you see it. Post that picture someplace where you'll see it daily. See if you can look in the mirror and recognize that girl in you.

✓ How often do you apologize? What are you apologizing for? Do you mean it, or is it just something you say out of habit? Try an experiment to count how many times a day you apologize—or enlist a friend in a meeting or gathering to notice for you. See if you can track what's happening when you say it or if you're even conscious of it. When you've got some data and have tuned your ear to your ways, see if you can put the word "sorry" in cold storage for a day—and notice how hard or easy it is.

✓ How do you feel when you hear the word *brag* in your body? Do you wince a little or puff up? Regena Thomashauer and her work in The School of Womanly Arts says the ability for a woman to sing her own praises is directly connected to her power in the world, but it's a loaded concept because of the training we've had as women to be coy and quietly humble. Call it whatever you'd like—naming, claiming, tooting, taking a victory lap—but practice it. Celebrate your successes publicly as a woman—make some noise about it—and you will be doing us all a favor.

Resources for now or later:

✓ *The Book of Gutsy Women: Favorite Stories of Courage and Resilience* by Hillary Rodham Clinton and Chelsea Clinton
✓ *My Year of Saying Yes to Everything* TED Talk by Shonda Rhimes
✓ *Wolfpack: How to Come Together, Unleash Our Power and Change the Game* by Abby Wambach

+ *Half the Sky: Turning Oppression into Opportunity for Women Worldwide*, a documentary

Perspective

How Can I Keep Going?

THIS IS the place where tenacity and pluck can give way to sheer exhaustion and depletion, like a balloon that has run out of air after flying wildly throughout a room. It leaves you feeling collapsed and shriveled, hanging out with the dust bunnies under the couch.

Here is where pride in what you've done thus far can morph into fantasies of retreating—or perhaps back-peddling on your ambitions that now seem to feel "lofty" or "unrealistic." This is where you're tempted to cut your losses, call it a day, and dig a hole to crawl into and never come out again.

This is about the time you grow weary of people watching you— with admiration, envy, or concern—and start to feel a bit sunburned from being exposed to the intensity of their gaze for so long. Like the Grinch in Whoville, there are days you want to cover your ears to tune out the never-ending questions and comments that come your way. ("The noise…noise…ALL THE NOISE!") And then you feel guilty because you asked for this, right? And you should feel happy and grateful… except you don't in this moment.

You feel tired and spent. You've just tested your mettle and made yourself vulnerable again and again, and if you're honest, you're starting to feel a wee bit bitter and resentful that more people aren't joining you on this courageous path. Judgment can start to make an appearance here, and shame is quickly on its heels, like a remora riding in on a shark.

You might feel stalled, underwhelmed, unproductive, unfocused, lazy, or over-emotional—like your whole body is turned inside out for everyone to see—all of which has you wanting to play small and retreat inside yourself.

These are the moments where we forget that although we're in the midst of a deeply personal process, we don't need to do it alone. This is the place of restoration and renewal—of filling our cup, asking for what we need, receiving help, and getting a little perspective, validation, encouragement, maybe even permission to disappoint or recalibrate our expectations for ourselves or others.

But here's what I do know for sure: This is a blessedly human place—calling for new and different levels of self-care. Like a mountaineer arriving at a higher altitude base camp, there is wisdom in allowing time to acclimate before forging ahead with the next leg of your journey. It serves a person well.

18

A Woman of Intrigue

Remember when you were little and asked your parents for something that you *really, really* wanted? You knew it was a stretch and were afraid of what their answer might be, but you wanted it *so* badly, you asked them anyway?

Do you remember what they said to dodge the issue entirely and buy themselves more time?

We'll see...

I used to moan audibly when I heard that phrase tossed to me in the backseat of the car or when I was heading upstairs to bed. In my young mind, I believed that wasn't *really* an answer at all—it was... *nothing* I could use.

Like kicking the can up the road, it left me holding my big, fat desire for resolution in my hands a little longer, not knowing where it was going to land, when it would be decided, or if it was even worth my attention at all if I would ultimately be denied.

I wanted a black-and-white answer, and I got gray. I wanted to know what I should do with my expectations—were they realistic or completely outlandish? Did I have a snowball's chance in hell, or could I start telling my friends about my new toy?

What I know now, and that I couldn't have appreciated then, is just how fucking *brilliant* that particular phrase is — not just as a parent myself but also as a bold navigator in life.

"We'll see...." isn't the *absence* of a decision. It's actually a decision *not* to decide *now*.

Which is an extraordinarily powerful and useful tool if you want to stay open to where life takes you.

Because here's the deal, and I know you know this: We do *not* like to live in the unknown, so when someone commits to doing it, it makes all of us a bit panicky because we don't know *quite* what to make of you.

Like the kid wanting to know yes or no, adults are much the same way with their circumstances — we want black-and-white and get annoyed at gray.

We don't know how to handle someone who is in that liminal space — someone who's clearly on the way to somewhere but definitely has not arrived at a final destination just yet.

But lean in, my friend, because here's what no one talks about openly...especially Siri.

There *is* no final destination. There *is* no "there."

If we *really* want to get technical about it (and lots of people have tried to do this over the years, but do we listen? No...), the only thing we *really* have is "here." Everything else is "out there" and doesn't yet exist because we haven't lived it yet.

The sad truth is that most people living in the developed Western world suck at this—we just don't value ambiguity or see it as remotely productive or useful, and as such we've had little to no training in how to deal with it in ourselves and each other.

The present moment. Truly, that's *all* any of us can count on. This moment...then this one. And now this one.

That is a *key* piece of information to hold onto when you are travelling boldly and bravely through the unknown—and honestly, isn't that what we're *all* actually doing?

Aren't we all making this shit up as we go?

There are legions of people out there—*LEGIONS*, I tell you—who can't handle that concept. Scratch that: They can, but they won't. It would be too upsetting to their world because so many of us are wedded to this thing we call *control*.

And you, my friend, are out of it—in *their* eyes—not yours or mine. We know you're onto something, even if it feels hard and you question it most days.

You are wild. You have worked like a freaking wild woman to set yourself free from the trappings of your own mind. You have cleverly slipped your comfort collar, gone rogue, and given yourself unheard of amounts of permission and license to create.

You've trusted *yourself* like you never have before, despite your fears and in the face of your doubts. Who the *hell* do you think you are? What gives you the *right* to do that? Just what makes *you* so special? (She says with a sparkle in her eye...wink, wink...)

You've broken the rules, and that will be *deeply* concerning to many.

Because who are we without those precious rules of ours?

Many of us don't know yet. Some will never know. So this is your opportunity, woman, to show us how it looks as you go. This is your opportunity to show up as a leader of unknown territories, simply by letting yourself be seen.

I know you're probably still thinking you're in that liminal space and are far from "there," but you are *leading* us, even as you don't know where you're going—just by how you're choosing to show up and *be* with the unknown.

Do you see that? Do you get how powerful that is?

This is where I will remind women that we *know* how to do this *really, really* well, actually.

Think about—no, don't think, *feel*—these words as you read them, and then tell me women aren't absolutely *born* to embody these words:

Beguiling.
Mysterious.
Intriguing.
Flirtatious.
Magnetic.
Curvy.
Fluid.
Wild.

Think about seeing a really hot stranger across a crowded room and locking eyes with that person—maybe raising an eyebrow, just so.

You feel that? The playfulness of possibility? The power in not making a decision just yet? The commitment to staying open and seeing how it all unfolds?

This is how a woman physically embodies "We'll see...."

Terms like "feminine wiles" were invented for just this reason, so this is where I remind my clients to get them out, dust them off, and use them to combat the anxious onlookers.

I remind them you don't need to be "done" or have arrived anywhere specific to feel *confident* about where you are — and who you are.

I remind them of our power as women to express, *"Mind your own fucking business!"* in a way that feels flirtatious, disarming, and even charming.

I remind them that part of the package of *leading* from this place is to learn how to dance with the rubberneckers — because like it or not, people are intrigued by a woman wielding *that much power.*

This is witch work—unapologetically playing at the intersection of the material world and the magical realm.

Naturally people watch. Wouldn't you?

Remember the naked woman on the boat full of tourists, and how she didn't make eye contact with anyone? If you're just joining us now, check out pages 38-39...

Remember how the crowds parted for her? Remember how she

swiftly and effectively altered the *entire* culture of the boat simply by being herself without apology?

Remember how she didn't pay much mind to the onlookers and how they gradually concluded her nakedness wasn't such a big deal after all—even though it was?

That's what I'm asking you to tap into, woman.

The wisdom in your body that knows how to radiate "We'll see..." to others.

It's not *faking it* until you make it, it's not *lying*, nor is *hiding* behind a carefully contrived personal brand or story...it's just giving people something that will quickly turn down the outside noise and distractions that will inevitably come your way,

Being able to *focus* on yourself by being a woman of intrigue to others. Naturally.

Which, if you're getting my main point, enables you to engage with others while also buying yourself some time to figure it out as you go.

Imagine a hermit crab that has worked hard to slough off its too-small shell and is gradually making its way across the bottom floor of the ocean to find a bigger shell to call home.

Think about how tricky that traversing is for a little creature in a big open ocean. Imagine how vulnerable it must feel—oh wait, you probably *do* know, right?—and how hard it would be for it to focus on its journey if all the other sea creatures peppered it with questions (*"What's next for you?"*), caution (*"You've got to be careful!"*), and judgment (*"I don't know if that's a good idea..."*).

Being a woman of intrigue allows you to focus on movement by turning down the outside noise when you're in the unknown.

As a business owner, I do a lot of marketing. I could read books on how to do that, hire people to advise me, and do market research and focus groups, but honestly? I don't have the energy for all that shit.

Something wise in me years ago told me to tap into something I already had inside me.

What I've found — without really looking for it — is a way of being that feels incredibly authentic and also extraordinarily potent.

It came naturally to me and felt incredibly easy — even fun.

Vague, yet compelling.

That is how I work my magic with SheChanges. That is the phrase I tuck in between my breasts like a precious stone when I head out into the material world as a leader while also staying open to the magical realm to guide me, so I can find my way as I go forward.

Sadly, I used to mock this ability of mine, calling it *freaky* and dismissing it as something that was haphazard or quickly thrown together to get the job done. In all honesty, I used to call it *"pulling a rabbit out of my ass."*

But it was actually me, simply working my magic in my own distinctly feminine way.

I would meet with a woman who was going to be taking the stage with me at my SheSpeaks storytelling evening, and after half an hour with her, I could quickly grab three or four luminous threads and weave them into a description of her story — *long* before she actually knew what that story would be about.

"How did you do that?" she'd ask, marveling at how the description I crafted had the effect of her leaning in to hear more ("*I wonder what she's going to say…*") but also realizing it really wasn't saying anything too specific ("*I could basically say anything I want and it would still hold true!*").

My response? *Working my magic for the material world that is vague yet compelling…* It enlists the Muggle masses in your quest, without offering a lot of details that could box you in prematurely. It makes you stay open and yet seen.

Eventually, I realized it wasn't freaky or haphazard at all, this skill. It was *powerful* and something that women know how to naturally if we allow ourselves to tap into that ability more fully — as only we can.

One of my clients gave me the perfect illustration of what I'm talking about here. This was a woman who was deep into the unknown, actively seeking to work herself out of a job, while not knowing, exactly, what the next iteration of her professional work was going to look like or how it would all go down.

This woman wasn't about to get fired by others; she was actively getting desired by herself.

I witnessed her ushering herself closer and closer to that feeling of desire, taking another step each time she got more information until eventually, a picture started to form for her that was still vague but compelling enough to make her lean in.

Her husband was watching her do this over the months as well. He clearly trusted her, but he was also a bit worried as she was the primary bread-winner for their family. He wanted her to be happy and to follow where she was being led, but he was also wondering how, exactly, that might look — and when it would be done.

In a moment of clarity one day — that felt like she was emerging from this intensely personal trance of listening within herself — she realized she hadn't *really* caught her husband up on her latest thinking about things.

So she went home that night and pulled him — her flesh-and-bones life partner — into this dance she'd been engaged in with the unknown. She didn't offer him any clear answers or specific resolutions (she didn't have those yet), but she told him in a way that conveyed the *power* of her magnetism — the one that was actively turned on and pulling this new reality toward her: "This is what it's going to look like-*ish*," she said.

Did you catch that? Her "ish"? That's the key. Far from qualifying or explaining herself, she was offering a *bearing* for him to hold onto in the middle of the turbulent ocean, like one of those big red or green channel markers that keep the boats from hitting the rocks along the shores here in the coast of Maine.

Conjuring. Creating. And then? Enlisting.

Women do this *all the time* without realizing it. What do you think we're doing when we get dressed on those special occasions?

We're saying, "Look at me." Unless we're not.

Which begs the question: What are you saying to others when you show up publicly?

Are you dressing to be *seen*, or are you hoping to be *invisible*?
Are you dressing *you*, or who you think you're *supposed* to be?
Do you feel powerful, or are you concerned we can't handle you?

A woman's body is her primary tool of creation, so it would make sense that adorning it — literally (with our clothes) and figuratively (with our words and how we carry ourselves) — is an opportunity to use what we've been given more fully with all our distinct curves, roundness, colors, and scents.

The opportunity here is to maintain focus on yourself during this transition at a time when the noise from others will likely increase. The invitation is to embody yourself fully, publicly, while you are *still* in transition, and author your own narrative in a way that allows yourself to be seen without giving away your power.

Ultimately, it's also about relinquishing control of how others perceive you.

It's about rethinking our commitment to that whole idea of follow-through and that old rule (who said that, exactly?) of "*Do what you say you're going to do.*"

It's about giving yourself boatloads of permission and holding brave and important space for yourself to change your mind — or direction, outfit, desire, plans — as you go, so you can stay open to new information as it comes your way.

It's about you being fluid, not rigid— especially when it comes to expectations, your own or others'.

Are you sure you know what you're doing?
Don't you think that's a bit much for you?

Is that really the wisest choice?
Have you thought this through all the way?
Aren't you setting yourself up to fail?
Are you sure this will make you happy?
Don't you think that's a bit unrealistic?
That doesn't sound too practical...
Maybe you ought to rethink this...
I'm just worried about you...
What will people say?
What if it doesn't work?
Are you sure you're not making a big mistake?
Do you think you'll regret this?
Do you think this is a smart idea?

Do you hear that? Do you feel that in your body?

That's the sound of deflation — like a big red balloon losing all its air, dashing all over the place with that high-pitched noise.

Can you imagine being moments away from climax when someone starts asking you all these questions? Yeah, good luck with that.

Don't let your balloon deflate, woman. Not after all you've done to fill yourself up.

"Everyone keeps asking me what I'm doing, what's next, and when it'll happen...and I have no idea. I just feel like such a loser." And she sighs.

One of the hardest things about leading (yourself or others) during a transition is dealing with all the shit that comes your way — questions, concerns, advice, judgment, feedback.

Something I've found immensely helpful in this place is having a handful of "back pocket" phrases at the ready that help you tap back into that *Woman of Intrigue* place that keeps you rooted and steady while you're standing naked on the deck of the boat.

You'll know you've hit on the right ones for you when they fall into that "vague yet compelling" sweet spot I referenced above. It's the place that lives between not telling the complete truth but not really lying either. Here are some of my favorite go-to phrases that my clients and I reach for:

Wouldn't you like to know!
We shall see...we shall see...
Well isn't that the question of the hour?
I guess you'll have to wait and see, won't you?
The answers, my friend, are blowing in the wind... (sing that one)
You'll just have to wait for the big reveal to find out...

The key here is the use of humor and not giving anyone any specifics, you getting that?

I will say, it's amazing how quickly these statements shut people up and move them along without feeling offended or somehow out of the loop. On the contrary, it has the effect of giving people the impression they're now somehow in on your *secret plans* — like they're part of know, even though they know absolutely nothing more than they did before.

Think about it: People like to feel special — as if they are part of someone's inner circle where there are inside jokes and mysterious looks of understanding exchanged.

The genius part of this is that these people now become unexpected allies of yours — like they are part of your own secret service, devoted to keeping it safe until you decide to reveal it yourself.

Being a woman of intrigue is powerful shit.

Tap into it and see for yourself. It makes things a helluva lot easier when your energy is low, the distractions and noise are high, and you've got nothing left to give.

Focus, woman, focus. Be a woman of intrigue to them so you can focus on you.

What I know for sure:

✓ There is a physicality that is required to live in the unknown as you make your way from here to there, which can be taxing and distracting during a time when you are trying to focus. This is compounded by the vulnerability you feel as you start to break rank, stray from the pack, and head down the path not taken. The space around you can start to feel congested by nervous onlookers and people hungry for some drama or excitement — like rubberneckers that slow down on the highway when there's an accident. This is an odd little quirk about our human nature and not necessarily about the "accident" itself.

✓ I marvel at how frequently questions can be convenient vehicles for other things besides curiosity — like judgment, concern, envy, fear, criticism, insecurity, or skepticism. Likewise, I marvel at what a useful tool humor can be in these instances, to both defuse the tension and discern the ravenous onlookers from the truly compassionate witnesses. The difference can be felt from the nervous laughter from the cheap seats and the knowing silence of those with experience in the arena.

✓ Being overly rigid and structured isn't conducive to transition and can staunch the flow of valuable information and insights at the time when you need them most to guide you. It's important to be mindful of locking yourself into any commitments or expectations that feel like they might constrict your flow. This is the place where your inner world is rich and multi-colored with possibilities but has not yet been fully formed, so see this as a private season and opt out of things that feel noisy, invasive, or arduous in nature.

What helps:

✓ Dressing the part of a woman of intrigue is not to be underrated. See yourself as the leading lady of the main feature and take care to outfit yourself accordingly. If intrigue is the look you're going for, then give the people what they want with ruby red lips, an armful of bangles, and a brilliant scarf to tie the ensemble together. Thigh-high boots and a cape wouldn't hurt. But dress your intrigue from the inside out.

✓ Practice walking fluidly, moving your hips side to side, rather than keeping them facing straight forward. It's like the difference between a forced march on a cold, wet day and a sultry sashay on a balmy evening. Guide your body the way you want to move, and your weary head will follow its lead. Favor slow and present over fast and purposeful.

✓ Craft a narrative about what is happening these days for you, so that you use the power of your pen to author your own life and don't leave others to make it up for you. Make a list of some "back pocket phrases" that don't say much but do the trick (my two favorites are *We shall see....* and *Wouldn't YOU like to know...*) when people come at you with all their questions and desire for details.

Resources for now or later:

✓ *Fed Up: Emotional Labor, Women, and the Way Forward* by Gemma Hartley
✓ *Boundaries and Protection* by Pixie Lighthorse
✓ *The Secret Desire in a Long-Term Relationship:* TED Talk by Esther Perel

+ *Unladylike: A Field Guide to Smashing the Patriarchy and Claiming Your Space* by Cristen Conger and Caroline Ervin

19

Does my sexiness upset you?
Does it come as a surprise?
That I dance like I've got diamonds
At the meeting of my thighs?
—Maya Angelou—

The Wholly Trinity

Growing up, we used to live in this really old apartment that I loved. My mom couldn't stand it, but she was in the middle of a really messy divorce, so she couldn't stand a lot of things, I imagine.

I was twelve and remember feeling like we were living in a treehouse, long before they would become cool and people would pay top-dollar to rent them on Airbnb. No, this was more of an *accidental* treehouse, one that small rodents and spiders saw fit to claim as their own.

At night I would lay in bed, smiling with delight as I listened to a red squirrel roll nuts down the inside of the wall. Starting up high, he'd roll it one way, and then you could hear it drop to the next level, and he'd roll it back the other way until he worked his way down the wall. It made my mom shake her head with disgust, but honestly, I found it very soothing and rhythmical, reminding me I was part of the natural world, I suppose.

It wasn't long before I discovered where all those nuts ended up, though, because they all came tumbling out every time I reached for a sweater in my closet. Apparently, I had access to their stash of nuts, as well, and I saw it as a generous gesture that they entrusted me with this secret.

My favorite part of the house, by far, was the kitchen. Or more specifically, what *happened* on the kitchen floor each night. At the time, we had a fat cat named Nicki, and we kept his food bowl filled with Meow Mix, just underneath the overhang of the cabinets below the counter.

One night, we discovered that if you sat *really* still on the kitchen floor and waited *really* quietly, you'd soon see this little paw tentatively appear down from the space somewhere behind the cabinets, blindly reaching this way and that until—bingo!—his little hand landed in the cat food dish, at which point it would snatch up a piece and disappear. You could actually hear the sound of his munching coming from inside that unseen space.

We'd spend hours watching this little guy—who we could only imagine was a mole or some other small creature—and would torture him endlessly by shifting the dish just an inch or two to the left or right each time—just to keep it interesting.

I'd think of this mole many years later, reaching around blindly for some unseen morsel of food, because it felt like it perfectly described my relationship to spirituality and religion—constantly searching, with a frequently moving dish.

Because there came a time when I needed what was in that spiritual dish.

I went to go pray, and much to my horror, I had no idea what I believed—about anything. I had been raised in a bit of a hodge-podge fashion spiritually-speaking, attending whatever church we were going to at the time on Easter and Christmas Eve, getting confirmed (whatever that meant...), and being insanely jealous of all my Jewish friends who got to go to Hebrew school every Thursday to learn how to read backwards.

I hear versions of this same story with women all the time—the seeking, those hollow obligations (or shame, resentment, even trauma) of our youth, and this unnamed hunger at the times we feel most untethered and lost.

I resisted playing in this realm with my clients for years, until it became undeniably in-my-face relevant—and key to my work.

Ever heard of a leap of faith? That's where spirit comes in.

That last bit: faith. That is a key piece of the puzzle, it seems, and women are hot on the trail of it, even as I continue to hear unbelievably sad and horrid stories about "recovering" from their particular familial indoctrination into this world of religion and matters of the spirit.

Before engaging in this conversation, these women were careful to clearly delineate the difference in their minds between *religious* and *spiritual*, and I learned a lot from them about why that is an important distinction to make.

Religious transported them instantly to the world of doctrine, obligation, shame, mindless recitation, repentance, being unclean, underrepresented, and being the source of original sin. Just giving voice to their experience and speaking honestly made them feel like they were betraying something fundamental but not truly theirs.

Spiritual transported them to this expansive world that encompassed a broader landscape that included nature—animals, seasons, the elements, celestial bodies, more organic rhythms, journaling, meditative practices, music, art, dance, and their senses.

Do you feel that difference in your body over there? How one is a more masculine construct (organized, structured, predictable), while the other is more feminine in nature (wild, organic, and constantly changing)?

It's not that one is better than the other. We're not talking about right and wrong here, we're talking about this:

Food for a woman's soul.

And the women I know? They're hungry — starving, even — for the food that the spiritual world offers them, and they are starting to root around just as I had been, looking for a food bowl that would offer a morsel of sustenance to carry us through.

While they missed the taste of many pieces from the past— like community, rituals, scents, silence, and the thoughtful reflection that happened within it—they were no longer willing to fit themselves into a narrow box in order to access it.

These were wild women, no longer content to be contained.

Remember that "puzzle" I referenced up above? It wasn't long into my work with women that I started to notice there were *three* consistent topics that kept coming up for these women navigators charting their course through open water.

These three pieces would often be bundled in the same package together, and this package had a name:

"Balance"

Over the years, after witnessing many, many women unwrap this very same word for themselves—because what does that word even mean, do we know? —it became clear that this concept of balance was really a bucket that held these three things:

Our spirituality, our creativity, and our sexuality.

How each one of us defines those concepts will be different. But however a woman chooses to define them for herself—and that's often part of the work I do with them—I have been amazed by how consistently these three concepts kept showing up *together*, like a team.

When a woman was really connected spiritually, she found she was turned on sexually—her body seemed to come alive from within—her senses woke up, and she felt more magnetic, radiant, and sexy as a result.

When a woman was feeling strong and deeply connected to her body through movement or intimacy, she quickly found her creativity would go off the charts because she was so inspired.

When a woman gave herself the freedom to completely immerse herself in her art or creative endeavor, she felt like a force of nature and incredibly powerful, like she was plugged into something bigger than herself.

You see what I'm getting at? These three arenas—our spirituality, our creativity, and our sexuality—are integrally connected for women, like magnets, they are drawn to each other naturally.

It's why I call them The Wholly Trinity.

It was most present for me at one of my women's circles years ago when we gathered on a bleak February evening to tease apart this concept of "balance" with each other.

In a moment of inspiration, I flipped to a clean piece of paper on an easel pad and started sketching out what I had been noticing among my clients. I drew an inverted triangle, writing one of these three topics on each corner of the triangle.

I then went on to give example after example of how women tapped into these for herself, and how they seemed interrelated, as a way to offer flesh to the bones of this concept I had been playing with in my practice.

Flushed and out of breath from talking so quickly, I turned back to the group of seven women who had gathered that night and asked, "So what does this have to do with the topic of balance?"

Big, long silence. And then one woman laughed out loud and said this:

Well, shit. Who the fuck needs "balance" if you could have *that*?

It seems we had hit pay dirt.

But the key to remember here is that this is a really *personal* — and often *private* — conversation for a woman to have with herself, and it asks a woman to stay open to being surprised, and yes, even delighted, when something unexpected or unfamiliar falls into her path.

Here's an example of how that looks from my own journey.

At my Homecoming weekend women's retreat one year, this woman approached me on the second morning and said to me:

"I have a message from Jesus for you."

I knew this woman well because I'd worked with her the previous year. She was a deeply Christian woman, and her faith was often at the heart of many of her desires and decisions in her life.

So, when she said she had a message from Jesus, I damn well believed she did. Moreover, I wanted my message.

I said, "Cool! What did he say?"

She went on to tell me that Jesus wanted me to know that my work was deeply spiritual, even if I wasn't really seeing or believing that just yet.

I remember that comment landing inside my body as truth. I nodded like, *message received*, and thanked her as she quietly walked away. As I stood there that day, I could feel more of my old consultant skin stretching tight as it cracked and started to slough off, without my permission. And I silently thanked Jesus for my message, even though I'd never met the guy.

But I am reminded of that same sensation in my bones — opening to the unknown and the discomfort and vulnerability that comes with it — every time I hear a woman say to me that she doesn't know if she believes in all that "hippie-dippy stuff..." then lean in a bit with, "But tell me more..."

It's okay — and natural — to have that reaction, but lean into it anyway, because as I've said countless times before:

Your body never lies. So follow where it leads, woman.

Want to know how that looks?

It's going to be up to you to define that for yourself, but to blow on the embers of that fire within you, here's how I've seen other women ignite themselves over the years:

One client decided she wanted to get up every day for a year and do a quick sketch of the sunrise.

Another woman chose to doodle and make art on a page of *Women Who Run with the Wolves* each day, as a sort of artistic meditation, noticing which words jumped out at her on the page and playing with them all day.

One woman took an online course to learn about the power and practice of using Yoni Eggs (Google Rosie Rees or Layla Martin).

Someone else decided to adopt a Morning Pages practice as outlined by Julia Cameron in *The Artist's Way*.

Another tore up her backyard and decided she was going to grow her own vegetables.

Another woman decided to sleep naked for a month and take up the entire bed.

One woman visited a sacred feminine site she had driven past countless times, and she was overcome with her own desire to put her naked breasts to the earth in communion.

One woman started using fine china, crystal glasses, and the good linens for dinner with herself, effectively making herself her own special occasion.

Another woman surprised herself by giving in to her urge to bury some of her menstrual blood in the ground each month when she cycled.

Someone else took selfie pictures daily and posted them on social media, so she could be more mindful of how she was choosing to adorn and outfit various parts of her spirit and personality.

Another woman challenged herself to see if she could write a novel in a 28-day moon cycle (Google Write a Book November).

One woman decided she wanted to reclaim the practice of rosary beads, but on her own terms and in her own way, by stringing prayer beads and meditating with them daily (Google Simply Pray).

One woman joined the chorus at her church and ended up forming her own women's singing ensemble that gathered at each full moon.

Many women have participated in Mama Gena's experiences as a means to understand their relationship to pleasure and their bodies — and then turn it on more fully (see resources below).

One started taking pictures of the clouds because she found herself so often traveling in airplanes for work, and it had her reconnect with something greater than herself.

Another woman decided to organize and design a "croning" ceremony for herself, inviting the closest women in her life to gather in her honor one evening and witness her rite of passage.

Still others have discovered the meditative practice of OM-ing (google Orgasmic Meditation) as a way to enlist their partners in their experience and practice receiving.

Many women have sheepishly confessed that Mary Magdalene has been finding them to talk — through their writing, dreams, and walks in the woods.

Plenty have used their kids as convenient inspirations to get on this themselves, making meals together, checking out a different spiritual community each week, going skinny-dipping on vacation, or getting on the floor and making art with them.

Still more have given themselves full permission to undertake wildly new and creative projects, like building a shed, renovating a home, or a refinishing piece of furniture.

Are you getting the picture — or some ideas — here? All different, all personal, all surprisingly nourishing things they might not have seen coming or allowed themselves to have ordinarily.

And that's what we're talking about here— the ordinary days.

Most of us can find a way to rise to the occasion of the *extraordinary* days — those moments something big happens (we get fired, we close the sale on the house, we finally ask for a divorce, we register for the course, we buy the ticket).

But what about all the days in between those moments when our exhaustion gets the best of us, and we start to wonder what the hell we were so excited about, like rushing upstairs in the house to get something, only to wander from room to room, saying out loud, "Why did I come up here, again?"

Those are the moments we can reach for any *one* morsel of food that lives within the Wholly Trinity — because it reminds us that we can get to the same place and access that same nourishment for our women's souls through any of the *three*.

Keep reaching your paw out for the Meow Mix bowl, even if it moves on you time and time again. Grab a morsel and eat when you can.

The care and feeding of the Wholly Trinity of your power as a woman are yours to assume, so keep finding out how that looks and feels for you.

You don't have to find God, seek out a guru, or apply to Harvard Divinity School to get your masters in feminist theology, although those might be appealing to you.

It's not necessarily about having more sex, learning about female ejaculation, or buying a crystal wand, although certainly, those might do it for you.

Please hear me that it's not about registering for the New York City marathon, training for an Iron Man, or getting lean and chiseled doing Cross Fit, although that might be of interest.

It's about learning to fuel yourself through the ordinary moments.

The moments when the inspiration has faded, exhaustion has set in, and you're feeling most alone, crazy, or lost.

This generally happens in the dark of night — the witching hours, the very time women start to bleed naturally in their cycles — when the world is most quiet, and there is nothing to distract you from your own thoughts and feelings.

Your body will be your best ally here because she will let you know if you're on the right track. If it feels good to you, you are.

It's all about how it makes you feel in the moment—if it tastes good to you, not to someone else.

I'll leave you with this one final thought—like a heritage tomato seed passed among women in a community garden, this particularly juicy one was offered to me by a dear friend:

"If our bodies are sacred, then sex is worship."

My friend Jeanne concluded her story at my SheSpeaks storytelling evening with this, casting it out to the audience like a beautiful golden net that fell lightly over us.

And then she sealed her spell by telling us to all to go home and have *really good sex* that night. Witch's orders, I presumed.

Find your way home and make love, woman. Begin with you. Again, and again.

What I know for sure:

✓ No one can tell you what feels good in your own body, or if
something feeds your own soul—so that is on you to own
or not. You'll know it's right for you if it feels good, even if
your brain is telling you otherwise. Bodies, like any operating
system or transport vehicle, need certain things to operate
optimally. Far beyond water, food, and safety, I'm talking
about joy, vitality, and intimacy. The first set will support a
being functioning in the material realm, while the latter set
will support a being harnessing the full power of what is in the
magical realm as well. Your body is your instrument. Use it.

✓ We are sadly really conditioned to expect pain, and as such
we have been well trained in knowing how to respond to it.
If you listen to the stories of women, they will often gravitate
to the ones that focus on *overcoming* something hard or being
resilient in the face of struggle. They rarely are about stories of
pleasure—we are taught this isn't as noble or worthy, and so
we resist it, dismiss it, or shame it. We love adversity stories
but openly mock romance. I believe it's critical to the health
and wellbeing of women—not to mention the harnessing of
our full power—that we change this narrative for ourselves
sooner rather than later.

✓ To engage in this conversation with ourselves—and
each other—as women will require an open mind and a
willingness to entertain things that feel non-traditional,
wildly uncomfortable, and/or contrary to our existing beliefs.
Which means your head will inevitably have *lots* to say about
the matter, and you can expect lots of internal chatter and
questions. It will also test the limits of your ability to receive
the good stuff in life (pleasure, ease, grace, serendipity) as these
areas start to open you up to access and work your magic as
a woman.

What helps:

✓ Take an inventory of what gives you pleasure. Make a list, the simpler the better. If you get overwhelmed, begin with your senses: What tastes good? What feels good to your skin? What sounds good to your ears? What smells good to your nose? What delights your senses? Raise your consciousness by having a list at the ready and maybe post it on your fridge or mirror. Sometimes that's all it takes. Think of the metaphysical law: *Where attention goes, energy flows.*

✓ Build an altar. Again, watch for your brain wanting to make this a big, hairy deal. Think in terms of devotion and love, instead of any particular deity or spiritual practice or purpose. Fill it with things that feel meaningful to your heart and soul, like a heart-shaped rock, a candle, a jade yoni egg, or a blank journal. Don't make it a one-time event but a work-in-progress — always — that you add to and change up depending on your moods and seasons. See it as a placeholder for your spiritual conversation with yourself.

✓ Bring color into your world and get physical with it somehow. Paint the wall in your kitchen a color that makes you squeal with delight. Plant a garden. Refinish that old chair in the basement with new stuffing and a brightly colored fabric. Create a vision board with magazine pictures, poster board, and glue sticks. Get your hands in it and play.

Resources for now or later:

✓ *Making Life Easy* by Christiane Northrup
✓ *The Dance of the Dissident Daughter* by Sue Monk Kidd
✓ *Pussy: A Reclamation* by Regena Thomashauer

+ *Orgasm: The Cure for Hunger in Western Women*, TED Talk by Nicole Daedone

20

Joy & Other Metrics

On a ski trip with our boys up in Canada one winter, I got a lesson in relativity.

After a long day of being outside in nature, we decided we would ski four more runs as a family before heading in for the night, each person choosing one that the rest of us would go on, like it or not.

My youngest son chose to go down *The Enchanted Forest*.

We had gone by the entrance of this run on several occasions, and I thought it looked fairly benign as it disappeared into the woods, underneath a brightly colored sign with woodland creatures and happy looking children. Each time we'd ski by it, we could hear the bells and gongs coming from inside, giving us the sense of how the trail lived up to its name.

So when it came time to head into the Enchanted Forest and ski under that happy-faced arch, I wasn't anticipating the hell that was waiting for me.

As my two boys zipped high and low over the hills and dales, gonging the bell and whooping with delight, their little bodies attached to their short little skies, I met with a much darker fate.

Enchanted, my ass—that place was fucking haunted.

Within one turn, I was doing my best imitation of one of those witches on brooms people attach to trees—you know the one where she has a leg on either side of the trunk, and all you can see is the back of her witchy head?

That was me. Only picture me swearing like a sailor, frightening all the little children going over hill and dale around me.

It wasn't even that long of a trail, but it seemed endless, dipping around turns and dashing us through the snow with an alarming amount of speed and trees, trees, trees everywhere.

Eventually, I gave up the fight and pointed my skies deliberately into the woods where I knew my familiar non-enchanted trail was waiting for me on the other side like a loyal friend.

Soon enough, I hit a tree, grabbed it hard, and sat down, cursing the asshole at the ski resort who was responsible for signage, and how he didn't see fit to depict even a few faces of sheer terror on that magical arch that would have made me think twice.

Now my sorry ass was covered in snow up to my hips, and I had to crawl through the woods to get myself out of hell, shamefully dragging my skis behind me.

It was not my finest moment.

But isn't that the case so often—something that seems so benign and simple to one person can be so challenging and terrifying to someone else?

That whole experience really called into question my relationship with blue squares—that large and sketchy categorization for ski trails that falls somewhere between the beginner green circles and the advanced black diamonds. Up until that point, I had trusted blue squares to guide me.

I was second-guessing what I was told. Everything had changed, and I didn't know who or what to believe.

I had a similar experience earlier that fall when I decided to sign up for a half-marathon trail run. I had done one a couple of times before, but the idea of doing it in the woods sounded, well, like an *enchanting* idea.

The day of the race that October morning was unseasonably cold with an incessant rain coming down and no hope of it ending soon. Just that week, the leaves had finally fallen from the trees, so I knew the woods—and any trail in them—would be thoroughly carpeted in wet leaves, making it a bit treacherous to navigate.

I'd never run this particular race before, and I wasn't running it with anyone—just me—so while I was pinning on my number, I looked around to see if I could find a map that might orient me to the trail system.

It turns out it was one of those late-season runs, where everyone seems to know someone else, and most were familiar with the course, having run this race previous years.

I hadn't, though. And it made me wonder what I might have signed up for. Thirteen miles covers a lot of ground in the woods— enough to get lost, and certainly ample opportunity to, say, trip on a root and dislocate the shoulder you'd be keeping in its socket successfully for the past thirty or so years.

I caught the eye of a woodsman-looking guy, filling up his mug by the coffee urn. He clearly wasn't going to be running this race, or if he was, he was not dressed appropriately.

He was rather gruff and seemed irritated by my "Excuse me?" but turned around nonetheless.

I explained I was new to this race and wasn't familiar with the trails. I asked him if the half-marathon route was clearly marked. You would have thought I asked him if he was Big Foot's brother, the way he looked at me.

"Of course they're clearly marked," the thorny woodsman said, making it clear that he, in fact, was the one who had just spent all morning in the rain marking them—just for me, the idiot who didn't know her way—a task he clearly found ridiculous.

How inconvenient it must be to have the obvious questioned.

So sure enough, once I left the starting line with all the other runners, followed the crowd out to where the trail disappeared into the woods, I proceeded to get lost.

"Clearly marked," it seemed, meant itty-bitty signs tacked to a tree on this single-track trail every half mile or so. Signs that you'd really never see if you were, say, busy wiping rain off your face every minute and had to keep your eyes down, pumping your knees high like pistons to avoid tripping over tree roots.

But I learned a lot on that trail in the woods that day.

This path in the woods was not mine. I was following a path someone else had made long ago—someone who was native to these woods and knew them inside and out.

I didn't belong in these woods, and yet I found myself in them and needed to find my way out.

That's when this 13.1-mile run became less of a race and more of a moving meditation on the state of our world and all the "clearly marked" trails we have for people to make their way through it.

I had a reckoning in those woods about the directions and instructions we're given.

Unless they were created specifically with me in mind, they didn't really apply. In fact, they were worthless and sucked.

The runners who clearly knew where they were going that day in the woods were not only able to complete the race, but they were actually able to *compete* in the race.

These people were seen as focused, tough, efficient, and successful.

My group of runners may have been able to *complete* the run, but we were no longer *competing*. We were just doing our best to make sure we didn't fall or leave someone behind. We had to slow way down to stay safe and work together to find our way out of those woods, figuring the trail out turn by turn.

While the first group of runners was celebrated, it felt like our group was merely tolerated. We weren't taken as seriously in that race, and we became practically invisible as the crowd thinned and people packed up and left.

And yet, that half-marathon will always hold a special place in my heart as one of my all-time favorite races. Why is that?

Because I had a lot of time to think in those woods that day, and I learned a few things that I pocketed for later about how I—and others—define success. It's not a one-size-fits-all sort of deal but a deeply personal conversation.

It's critical to decide for yourself your own measures of success—otherwise, you'll rely on someone else's.

It reminds me of something my nonagenarian father-in-law said one day in the kitchen of their farmhouse, when I came in and saw him eating this god-awful looking dish that was basically grated carrots floating suspended in pineapple Jell-O. I wrinkled my nose and asked him if it was any good.

"It's good if you like it!" he responded quite simply.

So those rules, and markers on the trail and measures of success? *They work if you make them*—because measures are relative to the makers, not the followers.

The tricky bit, though, is that nasty conditioning we have as women to compare ourselves to others—especially other women—when we're feeling lost in the woods of life, are worried about tripping on roots, or are exhausted from pumping our legs like pistons.

Curiosity is the antidote to comparison.

"Why does it feel like I'm the only one who needs to go on this discovery process?" she asked.

My client had come to me for the same reason so many of them do— she just had this sense there was more in her, but the comfortable familiarity of her current business was keeping her from exploring what else she might do. She had this story about something being wrong with her.

In her mind, everyone else already figured out what they were looking for — answers, clarity, passion, vision, a map, confidence, a plan, clarity — but she needed help. She felt like she was late to the party or had missed something everyone else had gotten long ago.

The bottom-line was that she thought everyone else knew something except her, which left her feeling vulnerable.

I hear this a lot, and I get it. I do. It's what we're trained to do when we are feeling alone, insecure, scared, and lost: compare ourselves to others. I've fallen prey to this more times than I can count, and my clients have, too. It's natural and human.

A case could be made for it being part of our humanity. We are, after all, creatures with a primal urge to belong, so when one of us strikes out and goes rogue — breaks the rules and makes her own — sometimes that sensation of loneliness comes as a surprise.

But curiosity is the way out of this state, not a death sentence.

You know that saying we heard so often when we were naturally inquisitive kids: "Curiosity killed the cat"?

What does that even mean — have you ever stopped to think about that? Did it *really* kill the cat? If you look that particular phrase up, here is what you will find:

A proverb used to warn people against unnecessary investigation or experimentation.
An expression used to warn someone not to ask too many questions about something.
Being inquisitive about other people's affairs might get you into trouble.

There are even links in this phrase to a woman's sexuality, suggesting that this is what happens when a woman gets screwed over one too many times by a man, that she somehow "kills the cat" by finding greater satisfaction by bedding another woman and "becoming a lesbian."

It seems this is about our relationship to our wildness—our superpower—as women.

Much like women, there is tension between cats being inherently wild and independent creatures by nature, and how we have sought to systematically *domesticate* them over time.

Sound familiar?

Like women, cats have long been associated with mysteries and fears — specifically, those things humans don't want to see and, in fact, can't see.

They are also associated with magic, a realm that flies in direct conflict with our Western values around logic, science, and anything concrete, rational, and proven.

It turns out, there was a massive disconnect in women's wires from all our power with that whole "curiosity killed the cat" nonsense.

The original saying — as I found with a bit more digging — was actually "*care* killed the cat" — "care" literally meaning "worry and sorrow" rather than our more contemporary interpretation of "looking after" or "providing for" something or someone.

It turns out it wasn't *curiosity* that killed the cat, but the true culprit responsible for its demise was simply *giving too many shits* about what other people thought about all that power.

Cats and women, it seems, are built to see in the dark and work magic—as long we don't worry about it. No shit.

One of my clients discovered this when she was talking about some of her regrets and biggest failures. This highly accomplished executive — someone most people would look at and admire — was talking about this deep shame she had for not getting into the college of her choice, despite getting top marks in high school and being a high achiever.

"That was my greatest failure," she said and got quiet, clearly still feeling the sting of that moment, now long in her past.

Moments before, she had been talking about the college she *had* ended up attending, and how it had been the *perfect* fit for her, both socially and academically. She lit up as she spoke, recalling how expansive, free, and full of herself she felt at that time.

So how is something that feels like a perfect fit for you a failure, exactly?

I reflected this all this back to her, asking her to elaborate on the failure part because she had lost me there.

She paused, and then she realized: *Her* perfect wasn't somebody *else's* perfect.

Up until this point, she had assumed she'd just made the most of a less-than-ideal experience of not getting into the college she wanted, but now she paused and considered the "failure" she had described.

She hadn't *failed,* she had *disappointed.*

In fact, the more we teased that newfound realization out, the more she appreciated how happy she had been when it worked out the way it did.

But despite the best of her best intentions, she had internalized that college experience as a failure because so many others had been let down when she didn't get accepted.

Her college years had been some of the happiest of her life. And yet all these years, she'd considered that whole chapter to have been a failure.

This is the power of defining your own metrics.

This realization has been a boon for my clients and me when it comes to creating change.

It requires us to assume greater levels of responsibility in defining our own metrics for things like success, productivity, and progress. And it asks us to be mindful of falling into the trap of what is "normal," conventional, or expected.

It's an invitation to make it personal—to shift from objective measures to subjective ones (with you as the subject).

Think about this:

How do you measure love?
What makes art successful?

How do you know a meal is productive?
What makes a garden worthwhile?
How does a baby succeed?
How do you measure joy?
What are the markers of progress in a friendship?

It depends, right? On you.

The trap I can easily fall into — especially when I'm tired, distracted, or feeling insecure — is to compare myself to how other people answer these questions.

I do what one of my favorite writers, Anne Lamott, cautions us against:

"Never compare your insides to everyone else's outsides."

I forget there is *no right* answer—just my answer, my experience, my truth. There's just what I know about doing me.

When my youngest was a baby, some new neighbors moved in next door who also had a son about the same age. Both parents were writers, and they tag-teamed raising their son while also working on their respective novels and teaching writing classes to students both near and afar.

In the heart of winter, house-bound and bored out of our minds, the mom and I would often find ourselves sitting on one of our kitchen floors together with mugs of coffee, talking about life while our babies pulled out all the pots from a nearby cabinet.

She was in the throes of writing her second novel, the one that would go on to be featured in *Oprah* magazine and rocket to success a couple of years later. But we didn't know that at the time. The only thing she knew is that she had stacks of index cards perched all over her kitchen counters, each with a particular character or scene from her book written on it.

When she had a quiet moment, she would lay them all out on the floor and move them around, feeling her way into this novel that was trying to be born through her. This was her process, and she knew it worked for her, but many times she lamented how messy, physical, and at times overwhelming it all was.

Some would say it was too much or crazy-making. And yet it worked for her.

Years later, after her book had been picked up, published, and met with more success than she ever imagined, I heard her reflect on the process of writing her book when she was invited to be on a panel discussion for writers. She spoke about how everyone thought she was crazy — hell, how *she* had thought she was crazy — to attempt to write a book while she was also trying to mother a young baby.

But in that moment, she smiled and said that she never would have been able to do it, had she not had the pressure of time and demands. In telling that one story, she raised a hammer and shattered the myth of what people might have assumed about her.

She showed herself as who she was — a woman who wrote a New York Times bestselling novel in her spare time on the kitchen floor of her apartment with a baby crawling around banging pans.

If she had listened to the way others told her to write a book, or if she had measured herself by how other writers' lives looked when they wrote, she might never have written that book at all.

Sometimes "crazy" is not really crazy at all, it's just inconvenient or non-traditional.

Plenty of people have looked at my life — who I am, how I show up, and all that I do in SheChanges — and thought they were somehow in a position to have an opinion about me.

I've been told I just need to relax, learn how to pace myself, not be so hard on myself, that I'm overdoing it, have too high expectations, need to pick my battles, don't do too much, cool my jets, and slow down...

To be clear? None of that shit is mine. I'm good with me.

I'm an intense person who is highly creative, highly ambitious, insatiably curious, and loves a challenge. Happily, I was also born with a nice, healthy dose of energy and the ability to recalibrate my own expectations on a dime if it all goes sideways.

It's also why I'm an entrepreneur because I do really well with lots of open space, tight deadlines, and knowing exactly what I will need — from myself and others — to get the job done.

I'm kind of done apologizing for being myself really well.

Monica Lewinsky learned a thing or two about how we make a blood sport of shaming each other back in1998, and she came to a really kick-ass conclusion seventeen years later in her TED Talk.

"Nobody gets to tell me I'm not a reliable narrator of my own story," she said.

You, as a reliable narrator of your life. Imagine that.

So, here's how that looks: Take the pen, decide how you define the terms of your life, be it happiness, success, balance, progress, productivity, or freedom.

Look through that lens of curiosity in all the areas of your life —
emotional, physical, professional, financial, mental, spiritual,
creative, social, romantic — and get more specific with your
definitions and measures of each.

Write that shit down so you don't forget it.
Paint your own signs.
Post your own trail markers.
Give other people's shit back to them.
Change your mind if you want to.
Finesse them as you live more into them.

If you take nothing else away from this book, I hope it's this:
Learn to do you really well.

Because if it's not your responsibility to do it, then whose is it?

Create your *own* Enchanted Forest.

And then ski down that trail with wild abandon, woman, ringing
the bell like mad and wailing on the gong with each new pass
through.

Show us how you do you, and we will all be inspired to follow
your lead — in our own way.

What I know for sure:

✓ In the absence of defining for ourselves what things like *success, happiness, productivity, balance,* and *freedom* look like for us, we will automatically default to the definitions set by others—which generally point us to how busy we are, how much money we make, what our title is, and how much stuff we own. Sometimes it doesn't occur to people that these terms are negotiable and able to be molded to better suit our values and our circumstances. They are not universal measures that are one-size-fits-all.

✓ When a woman goes rogue from "the way it is" and strikes out on her own, it tests not only her mettle but also her loyalty— to self and others. Because people are used to everyone being a certain way, the rogue woman will inevitably run into disappointment and confusion when it comes to her interactions with others. These are the moments when she is most tempted to betray herself—retreating back into the comfort of the known for the sake of keeping the peace with others. Change is a family affair, and there is a period of adjustment that takes patience and fortitude to navigate.

✓ There is a call to assume a deeper level of responsibility by the woman who enters uncharted territory, which is both a creative opportunity and an added investment of time and energy. What worked for someone back there most likely won't cut it as you're here, so this conversation *(What do I need? How will that look? When will I know?)* becomes a frequent occurrence rather than a one-time event.

What helps:

✓ Read up on people who inspire you or those who have taken the road less traveled or blazed a new trail altogether. Take notes from podcasts and interviews with pioneers, innovative thinkers, and trailblazing change-makers to see how they define, track, and measure their success. Permit yourself to color outside the lines of traditional metrics, and you will widen the range of possibilities.

✓ Assuming that the "way it is" is no longer appealing to you, then what will "your way" be? Put another way, what are your new rules of engagement (with yourself, others, and maybe your relationship to work/life), and what will be your new operating instructions that are aligned with and support you? Be the commander-in-chief and MFCEO of you and define your own parameters of how you will work in concert with your life.

✓ Keep an eye toward optimizing your life around how you are hardwired. Your brain might not like this exercise because it's asking you to consider more freedom to author your own life than you might ever have given yourself before. Design your life from an *ideal* perspective and get as *specific* as you can. What time of day are you most productive? What time of year do you feel most focused? Do you work in small little doses or intense deep-dives? Rather than twisting yourself into a pretzel because of how we've structured our world, give yourself a blank canvas and have at it.

Resources for now or later:

✓ *In the Company of Other Women* by Grace Bonney
✓ *Where Joy Hides and How to Find It* TED Talk by Ingrid Fetell Lee
✓ *Drop the Ball: Achieving More by Doing Less* by Tiffany Dufu

+ *Brave*, the movie

21

Flying Buttresses

I once attended a wildly different class designed and led by a lone wolf professor. I don't even remember his name, just the story of how he pitched it to the powers-that-be at Rutgers and because of his tenure or past successes, got the green light to try something new.

He was given the go-ahead to run an elective class called *Castles & Cathedrals* in a room that would hold twenty-five students. Fifty immediately signed up. The powers-that-be granted him a bigger room that would hold 75. Registrations continued to flood in, and the number of students interested grew to 150, so they gave him a small auditorium, and then a bigger one.

On the day the class began, I sat down among 500 students who apparently shared my gut understanding that this wouldn't be your ordinary class, that this—somehow—was going to be epic, an entirely refreshing approach to the normal drone and dryness of the lectures we had experienced in the past.

Something drew me into that class that day along with the 499 other students, and I had trusted it. I was about to get a lesson that would stick with me for my whole life.

The smallish, nondescript professor came into the room and chuckled as he looked up at the crowd that had gathered for his experimental elective class that didn't really count toward anything of substance in our degree programs.

He began by telling us a story that wove together all the threads I had been craving for myself in education — art, history, economics, philosophy, language, religion, culture, politics — as he painted a picture for us of why castles and cathedrals were so important to people back then.

This guy was going to show us how people had ultimately formed structures that would withstand the test of time — and be as beautiful as they were functional and sacred.

I was enchanted.

To illustrate how a cathedral was engineered, he said we were going to make one out of humans.

As he told the story of the paper-thin walls that were designed to reach far into the heavens and let in the light, he enlisted the help of eight volunteers from the audience and quickly positioned them in two rows of four people facing each other.

These people, he explained, were the walls of the cathedrals, and he had them lean in with their full weight to the person across from them and clasp hands, until their sixteen hands essentially formed the "roof" of the cathedral.

As he talked about the harsh environmental conditions at the time these cathedrals were being built — weather, changing landscapes, human impact — he took one of the students by surprise and pushed him gently (this was back in the early 90s when you could do that in a classroom) so that he lost his balance and bumped into another student, who set off a chain reaction among the group forming this human building. Pointing to the obvious instability of this structure, he then spoke about the necessity for flying buttresses.

He called up eight more students to be the flying buttresses, explaining how these added stability to the overall structure by widening its base on the earth and giving the thin walls added support to withstand the elements.

He positioned these people behind each person on the two walls, instructing them to lean in with their full weight on the lower back and hips of each wall person.

Then, in one glorious educational moment I will never forget, the professor launched himself off the ground and proceeded to swing like a monkey on the jungle gym of this human cathedral as the humans who made it up laughed out loud and barely budged, despite his best attempts to physically tax their structure.

I swear my mind took a snapshot that day, imprinting on my 21-year-old brain a visual of what it looked like to be supported by humans.

I noted the unabashed physicality with which this professor swung, trusting the design he had assembled. I noted the laughter and looks of joy on the faces of those who held up his weight, and how easy and effortless it all seemed to be.

Flying buttresses made of flesh and bones.

This image has kept me going on days when I feel most alone and vulnerable to the elements, so "out there" with my thoughts or actions that it feels as if one good gust of doubt or downpour of criticism could crumble my foundation.

When the fear of being toppled keeps me reluctant to lay that first row of brick.

There is an intimacy that is created between the walls of a cathedral and the flying buttresses that enable it to stand upright.

When they first come together, they are distinct parts of an elaborate design, but when the building is finally built, it all comes together as one breathtaking and structurally sound piece of architecture that is designed to stand the test of time.

Ancient, yet timeless. Ethereal, yet solid.

When I decided to strike out from the corporate world and design my own business, I remembered that visual and the lessons from that watershed class — those thin walls and how they needed support to remain upright.

Taking a page out of that professor's playbook, I enlisted the support of ten different women to play a specific role to buttress the cathedral of me I was building.

I chose each woman with a very distinct purpose in mind, having asked myself what I needed to feel safe, supported, and whole on this scary-as-shit endeavor I was undertaking. The list formed quickly in my mind, with topics like fun, spiritual connection, financial moxie, physical strength, strategic thinking, and badass activism rising to the surface. I considered who I knew in my circles that embodied each of these (or brought it out in me) really well, and one by one, I asked each of them to join me at my house one evening to gather as a group.

It freaked me out, making those asks, facing my fears of seeming selfish, self-absorbed, or (cringe) needy.

With each ask, I got more and more nervous and felt more and more self-conscious. And with each ask, I also watched as women rearranged their busy schedules, were flattered by my perception of them, honored by my invitation, and said a resounding *hell yes* time and time again.

I referred to them as my *Touchstones*, inspired by the idea of Stonehenge and how it must feel to be at the center of that massive structure as it buffered the elements in the verdant plains of southwestern England.

The first evening we gathered at my home, I was literally sweating. The kind of flop sweats that show in dark circles under the armpits when you gesticulate wildly, which unfortunately I tend to do insane amounts of when I'm nervous.

I had framed our gathering that night with a great deal of intention, which apparently was part of the allure to attend. This was not a simple social gathering or networking circle. It wasn't set up like a Mastermind group, in that there wasn't reciprocity designed into our group. No, this was all about me.

Sweaty pits. Liquid bowels. Lots of gulping.

As I spoke, I watched these women on the edge of their seats, alert and engaged, knowing this was something that took guts, felt scary, and was entirely intimate. I told them I needed their help for the next year, mapped out the six topics I wanted each one of them to help me hold — to physically buttress my intentions.

There wasn't a lot of small talk or idle chatter, only rapt attention on their part and sweaty palms on mine. They asked me a few questions, unearthing more specifically about how "help" would look and feel to me, and how I envisioned using them as a group.

I asked them to call me out when I was playing small or making excuses. I asked them to notice when I was fading or trying to make myself invisible—and to reach out and ask what I was hitting. I asked them to remind me that I didn't need to do this alone, and to ask for help and to point me back to myself when I stray.

My initial reaction to their suggestion of gathering monthly as a group was that I never wanted to put myself in this awful position again. It was hard enough to do once, why the hell would I bring this upon myself a second time? I declined, and they insisted.

Do the cathedral walls talk back to the flying buttresses once the master builder puts them in place? No, they do not.

The job of the cathedral walls is to reach high to the heavens, trusting they will be buttressed. They don't look down or back—just up.

So damn straight, we gathered again as a group at my home, at their insistence. And I sweat every time, but every time I also felt a bit lighter and a bit stronger as a result. Until I had forgotten they were even there, and their voices and presence became quieter and less visible in my life.

There came a time when I just *felt* them there, without actually hearing or seeing them.

I harkened back to this experience again when I set out to write my first book, and then this book, enlisting a group of twelve, and then six to be my "batch catchers" who would buttress my intention of writing in such a way that I actually began to produce writing each week ("a batch") that they would receive ("catch").

315

And like that first time, I cringed upon asking, and then relaxed into gratitude as I saw how my ask of them was graciously received — with reverence, honor, a commitment to be of service, and an unwavering belief in what I was building, even as it remained a mystery to me.

This is how it feels for women to support each other, even if we've been told or taught not to trust each other.

One dark winter night, I sat among a group of women gathered for my women's circle, and something remarkable happened.

We had been exploring the topic of "The Feminine" and appreciating just how *many* different ways we hold and embody this notion (or don't) as women. We had made a list of all the different "types" of women we were referring to as we qualified and explained our experiences of being a woman — *tomboy, girlie-girl, man-hater, earth mother...*

Our list was long and ugly, but it was honest and real.

After naming those different female stereotypes, we marveled that they were the *very* things that made us feel so divided — like hundreds of different boats all floating in the same ocean, in the same general place, but disconnected and feeling alone, judged, jealous, ashamed, or resentful.

"What if we all rafted up?" one of the women asked.

A delicious and thoughtful silence fell over the eight women gathered in my office that night as they considered this question, and then the sounds started, like primal moans and ancient hunger.

Oooooooo...
Ahhhh...
Mmmmmmmm...

This idea of *rafting up* offered a solution to our great feminine divide—enabling us to honor our *own* experiences while also supporting *others* who are traveling in different boats. Hope and excitement moved in—like a switch had been thrown—as we suddenly realized:

We didn't need to be *friends*.
We didn't need to *look* alike, *act* alike, or *be* alike.
We didn't need to *agree*.
We didn't need to *relate*.
We didn't need to *share* experiences and backgrounds.

We just needed to see that we were all together, floating in the same ocean.

We could be who we are individually and stay in our boat, but we could create a larger force for change simply by rafting up.

Many boats of women in the same feminine ocean.

There was something in that "rafting up" conversation which felt liberating—powerful, even—like we'd found the crack in the matrix of our cultural narrative that pitted women against women, creating more harm than it did help because of divisions, camps, judgment, comparisons, and criticisms.

What if we could stop focusing on our different boats and started focusing on the *entire* ocean that kept our boats afloat? What if we linked up and joined forces, creating a *massive flotilla*, a feminine armada?

No wonder we were making primal noises that evening. We knew we were onto something big.

Women working together is our only hope of creating change—and leading us forward.

Which means we need to look at our ideas of *sisterhood* a bit differently.

To move it *beyond* friends and getting along,
And move it *toward* witnessing and holding brave space.

To move it *beyond* fitting in and belonging,
And move it *toward* curiosity and broadening our perspectives.

To move it *beyond* expectations of long-term commitment.
And move it *toward* a desire for present-moment connection.

To move it *beyond* agreeing and disagreeing.
And move it *toward* challenging and championing.

To move *beyond* fixing, rescuing, or explaining.
And move toward listening, sitting with, and feeling.

To move it *beyond* a few women inviting others to the party.
And move it *toward* more women doing the party-planning.

To move it *beyond* talking about "us and them."
And move it *toward* talking about "I and we."

To move it *beyond* a main point and a bottom-line.
And move it *toward* what's outside the margins and at the intersections.

Women are capable of standing with each other in brave and naked spaces. And they are capable of holding multiple truths.

Now, this is where I'll pause and look more specifically at my white sisters. Draw near, white women, because we have some work to do here that our black, brown, and indigenous sisters have already learned to do by necessity.

We need to reckon with our white privilege — stat — if we have any hope of rafting up on this ocean.

Glennon Doyle spoke about this very thing beautifully in her story from Oprah's SuperSoul Conversations (see resources below):

"We cannot show up for the movement and say here we are until we say we are so damn sorry it took us so long. If our white feminism does not become intersectional, it will be nothing."

She said the beauty of this moment is that we were asleep and separate, and now we're awake and united — our collective pain has the opportunity to become our collective power.

We white women have much to learn about the role we play in perpetuating racism, and not only are we late to this party, but sadly, many of us are still reluctant to open our invitation to it.

We let the privilege of our overwhelm, our discomfort at being inept, and our shame at feeling the hard stuff keep us from reckoning with the gnarly root of how we show up as leaders — consciously and unconsciously.

Open your invitation and join me at this party, [white] woman — do your funky chicken dance or drag your white ass, it's okay. Bring your bags of shit and piles of nasty because I've got them, too. You are not alone, and we will do this together.

Here are some examples of how that work has looked for me:

✓ Participating in *Layla Saad's Me + White Supremacy Workbook*

✓ Educating myself about the history of institutionalized and systematic racism (check out *Racial Equality Institute*)

✓ Engaging in conversations with white people about white privilege—formally, informally, and frequently

✓ Listening, reading, watching, and learning from the stories, experience, and history as told by black, brown, and indigenous women through books, podcasts, interviews, and movies

✓ Noticing and naming what's hard for me to accept around white privilege, and where I tend to distance myself from it—making more space to feel, not explaining, defending, or soothing away.

✓ Learning the terms that black, brown, and indigenous people use to refer to the ways we white people engage or disengage with racism and our privilege: *white fragility, tokenism, white-centering,* and *emotional labor*

We can do the hard work to educate ourselves about racism and assume deeper levels of responsibly for the role we play in it. But let's do the work that's ours to do, so we lead from the whole of who we are with our eyes and hearts wide open.

Conversations of feminism must be intersected with conversations of racism.

Why? Because to address one without considering the other fails to acknowledge all the women on this beach, as we're all looking back at those raging fires.

And we need each other if we are to lead. We always have.

We know how to do this naturally. Think about it. Women gather informally at intersections all the time, talking, telling stories, and swapping ideas.

Climate Change + Healthcare
Childcare + Minimum Wage
Spiritual Beliefs + Leadership Practices
Women's Anger + Women's Service
Education + Privilege
Government + Industry
Mental Illness + Violence
Gun Control + Children

We do it informally and organically every day without even realizing it. But it's time we bring this more formally and strategically into how we lead.

What I am constantly unearthing and remembering with each new period of growth in my life is that we are stronger together.
We rise faster and better when we ask for help and enlist the support of others.

Our work in this world — whatever that looks like — is intricately connected to the presence of others. To ask for help takes an extraordinary amount of courage and to give it is both an act of service and a deep honor.

So, imagine us linking our arms on this beach as we all turn away from the houses on fire and burning shores to face the wide-open ocean as one. Imagine the cool breeze on your skin waking you up, while the warm arms of the women on either side of you let you know you're not alone.

That is us poised to lead together as one. We are here, with you.

A sisterhood of intersectional feminists. If that doesn't change the world, I don't know what will.

But it begins with witnessing each other more fully, just as we are, so we can buttress each other as we bravely lead toward the unknown.

It takes trust and courage—but not as much time, comfort, or context as we think. That's just a convenient excuse.

"How would you move if this were a prayer?" she asked.

Oh shit, I thought, rolling my eyes a bit at her question because I knew what was coming next. She was going to ask us to work with a partner, and I *really* didn't like to work with partners…

Couldn't I just do it by myself? Why did someone have to watch?

I groaned inwardly but listened to the instructions given by my lovely friend hosting this Qoya dance immersion she'd designed specifically to support women in harnessing the power of the new moon.

I wanted to stay open, even as I was really uncomfortable.

And, sure as shit, she partnered women up with the understanding that we would witness each other. But the really uncomfortable part?

Our task was to physically embody our desire in front of our partner.

What she was asking us to do was write the word each of us had decided upon at the start of the class — our intention — with our bodies.

No words. No explanation. No preamble. Just our bodies.

Fuck me. Fucketty fuck fuck fuck.

I had major intention remorse/envy in that moment. Why did I have to choose a work that was so looooonnnngggg? Why couldn't I have just chosen a simple one like *joy* or *love* or *fun*?

But my word? *Luminous.* Fucking luminous.

My partner was a woman I probably would have avoided, if I'm being honest, which made it all the more awkward. She seemed mousy and quiet, almost timid. The story I told myself about her was that she was a librarian or a medical writer for a pharmaceutical company. Maybe she was an insurance adjustor.

This is what vulnerability does to me — it makes me judgmental in an attempt to not feel what I'm feeling. Which is uncomfortable.

I went first because I wanted to just get this over with. Being dyslexic and a bit competitive, I "cheated" by writing my word down in front of me so I could reference the letters.

Did I mention we had to spell this work with our bodies both forwards *and* backwards? Um, yeah.

At first, I was very literal, wanting to make sure she could "read" what I was "spelling," moving my body like an upright snake to form each letter as this woman watched. That strategy got me as far as the first U in luminous before I got exhausted.

It was only when I closed my eyes that the magic happened. I felt myself drop deep down into my body, having each letter move up and through it, like a prayer or one of those paper lanterns released into the nighttime sky.

I lost all sense of time. I forgot my partner was even there. I wasn't aware of being watched, nor did I feel judged or worried about doing it "right."

I was all about feeling my way into this desire, letter by precious letter.

There was a fluidity to my movement, with each letter blending into the next, flowing both forwards and backwards seamlessly.

And when I opened my eyes, there she was in front of me: my partner, who had witnessed me working my magic. And her eyes were filled with tears — and love — as she looked at me.

It felt like this stranger was looking at my soul because that's what I had just given form for her to see.

Like magic, she had become a flesh-and-bones flying buttress helping me hold up my big intentions in the dark of night.

This is what women do, but more to the point, this is who we are quite naturally — it's why so many of us are midwives and hospice workers, enabling us to move over life's scary thresholds, just by supporting those vulnerable places.

Find your buttresses, woman. Invite them to your cathedral, tell them you want to fly, and then allow them to work their magic.

What I know for sure:

✓ Being supported by another human means we need to get much better about both *asking* and *receiving*, two things that are sticky wickets for strong, resourceful, and independent women. We often confuse needing help with being needy or weak, which is unfortunate — and also begs the question, "What's wrong with being in need or being weak?" What helps with resistance to this is to imagine you are the one being asked — for help or support. It's reverse-engineering empathy, putting yourself in touch with the joy of the giver, so you can feel willing to receive that gift.

✓ The concept of *Sisterhood* is not something that's talked about openly, frequently, or specifically enough and is often divided along racial lines, with black, brown, and indigenous women having their own sisterhoods that are wholly separate and distinct from white women (and from each other). Except white women rarely talk about our sisterhood, or if we do, it's assumed to be more global. The opportunity presented before us today as women is to redefine what sisterhood means — individually and collectively — in a way that honors our powerful differences as well as our common bonds.

✓ There is an intimacy that is present in women-centered spaces that is immensely powerful and deeply healing. Stories and information are exchanged freely, very little context or history is needed for a connection to be made, and there is a way of communicating that transcends the spoken word — expressed in a knowing look, the touch of a hand, or a silent nod of understanding. Women *get* other women, and when that happens it feels timeless and effortless, like magic.

What helps:

✓ See if you can view "reciprocity" as a *lifetime* opportunity, as opposed to a *circumstantial* obligation or expectation. Take the long-view and let go of any *shoulds* when you ask for support. The concept of "paying it forward" is a great tool to combat any fear or concern that arises. Open yourself to the possibility of repaying the gift you have been given, not to the *source* but to an unsuspecting person in need. See yourself in a long chain of people and keep it going — now or later.

✓ If you are a white woman, make the commitment to engage yourself in the conversation of your privilege using some of the resources below. Share what you're doing with others as a means to open the door and extend a hand. Know that our overwhelm, shame, guilt, and feelings of despair (Google *white fragility*) are indicators of our privilege at work and get curious about what lives inside them that keeps us from assuming responsibility for how we could be marginalizing people of color.

✓ Gather your women to talk about what it means to be a woman and why it matters. Share stories about how you were raised, what you were taught, and what you now believe. Listen, learn, feel, and notice how new, tender, and awkward this conversation is for many — and have it anyway.

Resources for now or later:

✓ *Me and White Supremacy* by Layla Saad
✓ *Makers: Women Who Make America* PBS documentary
✓ *We Should All Be Feminists* by Chimamanda Ngozi Adichie

+ *The Art of Asking*, a TED Talk by Amanda Palmer

22

"But still, like air, I'll rise."

—Maya Angelou—

A Middle-of-the-Night Letter

The heart of the night is always where my truth finds me—and sometimes it feels scary, as things always tend to feel bigger and more daunting when you can't actually see them.

I suppose that was the inspiration behind a request to help a dear friend of mine in her time of need. Her sister asked that the women attending her sister's baby shower include a letter sharing some of our lived experiences, stories, and hard-won lessons from the field of motherhood.

She explained that one day in the not-too-distant future, her sister was going to find herself awake in the middle of the night—worrying, doubting, questioning, beating herself up for something that happened (or didn't) in the very human experience of mothering—and she was going to feel so very alone.

Everything feels scarier at night—especially when you're the one leading and feel like you're supposed to know the way.

This turned out to be the best gift I have ever had the pleasure of giving. Truth be told, I would love a box of letters from my women to read on the dark nights of my soul.

327

But lucky me, I get to work with women every day who are *living* letters to my soul when I find I am weary, beaten-down, or lost in my own insecurities.

So this, my friend, is my letter to you when you're having one of those nights. We may never meet, but carry this with you in your pocket for safekeeping, or next to your heart, and know that you are *not* — nor will you *ever* be — alone.

• • •

I see you over there, Beautiful Woman.

You get to be tired. Of *course* you're tired.
You get to be riddled with doubt and insecurity.
You've never done this before — it makes sense.
You get to feel afraid — of course you do.
You're feeling vulnerable, which means you've stretched.

So, let's just sit here for a second — and not try to fix or do or "pull it together" so it looks all pretty and neat.

Because it's fucking messy and all over the place.

It's like those moments where you're "cleaning the house," but you get sucked into a particular closet that has been bugging the shit out of you for years, and so you start pulling EVERYTHING out of it into the hallway.

And then you look around, and the house that was messy to begin with now looks even worse with stuff strewn everywhere and piles of crap clogging the major arterials of your home.

That's generally when someone in your house will say, "I thought you were going to clean up...WHAT HAPPENED!?"

Those moments suck. So, let's just sit among the crap piles and talk.

Do you want me to tell you about all my crap piles? All the moments I've been caught red-handed by the people I love as I've been sitting and weeping in the big piles of nasty all around me?

What about the mistakes I've made and the balls I've dropped because I've been so distracted and self-absorbed by my own thoughts and feelings as I've been trying to unravel a thorny knot of fear-encrusted shit dusted with insecurity?

Or how about the comparing and judging I've done — and (gasp!) the mean-spirited things I've said as I've lashed out in those moments?

These are the moments a category-4 shame-storm can kick up in me. It might feel counter-intuitive, but do you know what helps? Make a pile of that shit — pull it out of the closet and add it to the crap pile. What's one more, right?

Let's start with fear because isn't that generally what's at the heart of it? Create a list of all the fears you've got in you. Start with "What if..." and fill it in with the concern or worry that's got you up at night. Don't worry about sounding "dramatic" or "overreacting" — I won't judge you — you should hear some of mine.

In fact, let me offer you those, lest you think you're alone. Some of my favorites are:

I'm worried I'm breaking the children.
What if people think I'm crazy?
What if I say something that offends someone and I'll never know?
What if I really am selfish?
What if I really am arrogant?
What if I'm full of shit and everyone is just humoring me?

Okay, so you get the idea. Now you try.

Notice how your body feels now? I just found I took a deep breath.

Your body knows. It never lies.

Bodies often don't give a rat's ass about being fixed or arriving at the right answer…they just want a fucking break and a chance to quit pretending there isn't a lot of shit they are carrying around inside.

Sometimes all they want is space to speak and the chance to have you listen — truly hear it — just so it can be acknowledged. It's where it's at with us women.

We all come from a woman's body — that's where literally everyone begins. That's the source. And we carry it with us wherever we go.

Women's bodies contain that source for us — so that's why I'm pointing you back to it, again and again.

And let me tell you something, sister, your brain will freak the fuck out the deeper and more frequently you trust that source.

Nothing about our society (yet…) has trained or prepared you to trust that source as real — but many things have conditioned you to fear it. You see that?

So feel me holding you by your shoulders and gazing directly into your eyes here on this dark night.

Trust as you've never trusted before, woman. Dig deep here.

Whatever has you worried or in your head, it's because you're close to something—and that something is probably a diamond in the rough, something valuable that hasn't yet been buffed and polished.

Good things—beautiful things—grow out of stinky shit in the dark of the middle of the night.

People who work with the land know this. Women know this. Animals and insects know this—why do you think dogs always stop to smell each other's shit? Good stuff!

If I were a betting woman, I'd say you're hot on the trail of something—something good, something important, something needed.

I know it sucks, but you actually don't need to know where it's taking you just yet.

Just keep following it. Sniffing as you go.

Think about Martin Luther King, Jr., and his dream…remember what he used to say?

You don't need to see the whole staircase; you just need to see the first step and take it in faith.

Yeah, that part: faith.

I have no idea the state of your spiritual affairs these days, woman, and honestly, it doesn't matter. But here's what does: believing in something greater than yourself. So, you know what helps in these moments?

Plug into the motherboard.

Do you remember what inspired you to start down this road, to begin with? Do you remember what it is that you believe? Do you remember the source of your hunger, where your appetite for this began?

Maybe it was a dream.
Maybe it was heartbreak.
Maybe it was this weird urging.
Maybe it was serendipity that delivered something to you.

But somewhere along the way, woman, you said HOLY SHIT, HELL, YES! to it.

I know it's late at night and you're tired, but do you remember WHY you said yes?

Put another way — and I'm going to get in your face a bit on this — see if you can recall why it even matters.

Why not just give up?

Change your mind! Forget about it! Fuck that shit! Let it go.

(Feel yourself holding on tighter to it? GOOD! That's telling...)

So why does it matter so much to you?

What I'm lovingly and fiercely asking you to do, woman, is FIGHT for it — whatever is inside you, please don't give up.

You've got something active on the line, and it's hooked. It's most definitely there, so now is not the time to pretend it's your imagination or — worse — that it's some sort of character flaw or personal shortcoming.

Truth be told, this is no longer entirely about YOU, my friend.

It's what you've got hooked on your line. Which is most likely about all of us.

So catch your breath, sure. And feel your feelings. Hell, you can even shit your pants if you'd like—no one would blame you.

But for all that's holy in the world, woman, do what you can to reel that big fish in for us. Go stand in some dirt and feel all that is good and holy and in need in the earth rising up through your legs and swirling around your big red heart.

You know how to do this, and if you've forgotten or you're too sweaty or tired to think, feel me and legions of other women on the deck of that boat with you reminding you of this:

Move your body.

No movement happens until your body moves, so sway it, shake it, shimmy it, stomp it, bump it, jump it, but MOVE it. Play some music, sing a song, beatbox, hum, dig deep, and bring out your Electric Slide or the Macarena. Do like Taylor Swift says and "Shake It Off." Strut with Nancy Sinatra's "These Boots Are Made for Walking." Ghost box with Kelly Clarkson's "Stronger." Swagger with Lily's Allen's "Fuck You Very Much." Take a stand like Cardi B. Go all *Footloose*, *Dirty Dancing*, or *Fame* on us, and we will join you laughing (and might pee a bit, but who cares?).

Ask for help.

Now is not the time to demure or play the cool cat—we can see you are working with everything you've got, and we want to lend our hands and hearts to be of service of you—and to whatever you've got on that line. It's not a bother, it's exciting to be a part of it. It's not selfish, don't be a friggin' martyr—martyrs just die, and where's the fun in that? We want you alive.

Talk to it.

Seriously, let what's on your line know that you see it, you're on it, and you're coming for it. Speak your desire out loud, and you will be casting a spell for us all to see and hear. Keep the lines of communication open, and you will maintain your relationship with it. Plug into being of service, and say a prayer (and it doesn't matter if or what you believe), dictate a letter, or send a voice memo into the great void — and then listen for some guidance, some encouragement that you're on track and right where you're meant to be.

Be clear on your intentions.

You don't actually need to know how and when all this will come to fruition, but it helps to keep your eyes on the prize by clearly and consistently stating your intentions — your *why*. The big stuff — the stuff that really matters to you. Is it freedom? Equality? Healing our planet? Putting more beauty into the world? Spreading love? Creating community? What is it that's driving you? Plug into that guiding light when you feel out of gas, and you'll get a boost.

Work with your rhythms.

Not someone else's road map. Follow the cycles and seasons of this path on your own. You can't always push or always rest, that's just not sustainable. A woman's body knows where to bear down and when to let up, so listen for that wisdom and trust it. It might not be what others would do or when they'd do it, but they're not the ones reeling this fucker in. Trust more deeply than you ever have — and honor what and when you are called to act upon.

Do YOU.

Put down the books, get off Google, get your nose out of your social media feed, stop asking people what they think, stop doing exhaustive research, running the numbers, doing risk analysis, comparing yourself to others, or shopping for a mentor a guru to teach you what they can't possibly know. DO YOU. You're the only one who knows how — and if you don't, now would be a really opportune time to figure that shit out by trial and error. The only way to do you is to embody who you are — to make you a verb by putting yourself in action.

Love up on yourself.

And if you can't because you're so bone-tired or you've never known how... ask someone else to. You are being super brave right now, extremely courageous — which is frankly more than most people can say on any average day — and if that doesn't deserve some love and affection, I don't know what does. You are smack-dab in the arena of your life, not in the cheap seats, so see if you can acknowledge what a fucking badass you are — even as you're covered in dust and shit and have tear tracks down your cheeks and maybe some blood on your legs. You're THAT woman.

See—and show—yourself as a leader.

Even as you feel like a crazy woman doubting herself — doubting everything — in the middle of the night. Because this is what leading looks like in a woman's body when no one is looking. Your courage, your exhaustion, your fear, your desire, your deep commitment to be of service, even as you are riddled with questions, overwhelm, or despair? This. Is. It. It just doesn't get talked about openly — or enough — in the light of day, where we see the outcomes from these efforts. But this is women's work: to bring what doesn't get talked about into the light of day. To not only embody who you are but also to give voice to why and how you do what you do. Begin by calling it leadership because honestly, woman, if it's not that, then what would you call it? You might not know it now, but someone is taking note of you — maybe it's your child, maybe it's an organization, maybe it's someone with a vote to cast or a dollar to spend — thinking: "Oh, so THAT'S what it looks like…."

On my darkest nights of the soul — when I'm up wondering what the fuck I'm doing and why I'm even bothering, questioning my own sanity and saying mean-spirited things to my curious spirit and its insatiable appetite or my badass warrior that seems eager for fight at every turn — I find my way back to where I started.

Remember those five questions that have been guiding us in this book, the ones that stand like our own personal Stonehenge on this beach where we've gathered? The ones that I've heard echoed time and time again in my work with women over the years?

Why me?
Why does it matter?
What's happening to me?
How do I do this?
How can I keep going?

Visiting any one of those questions — with genuine curiosity and an open heart — will bring me home to who I am as a leader. Holding sincere counsel with any one of those questions helps me find my footing when I stumble from sheer exhaustion, overwhelm, disorientation, or discouragement.

I remember who I am.
I remember why I feel so strongly about something.
I get a current read on what's living inside me.
I re-enlist and give myself deeper levels of permission.
I remember how I move best and honor that more deeply.

I ask for help and give myself greater levels of care and feeding.

All of that is in you — the questions just lead back to yourself when you drift, which you will, like the tides and the moon.

But if you're over there lost in the mousetrap of your mind, I'd offer you this gentle suggestion.

When you have those moments of disorientation or discouragement (or any dis-, really…), refer back to the descriptions I've written for each of the five sections of this book. I've lived through them so many times personally, and I have witnessed hundreds of women as they've done the same, and all that has helped to paint a fairly accurate picture of what you might be experiencing.

Which can be immensely soothing when you're in the thick of it — to know you're "normal," in good company, and actually on the right track. Finding some solace in those passages might offer a bearing on where you are at any one given moment, which is why I encourage readers to read this book in a non-linear fashion — to meet themselves where they are, not where I was or where you think you should be by now.

I know you feel alone — probably tired, and vulnerable, and maybe a little crazy, like you're losing it (or worse, have already lost it).

But I promise you, you're not alone. Somewhere on this big blue planet of ours, there is another woman sitting there in the dark, wondering the very same things you are, feeling the same emotions, maybe even wanting the same things. Imagine her with you now and know that you're not alone tonight — you just happened to be by yourself in this moment.

She is with you, as am I. Feel us.

Here is what I'll leave you with on this dark night, my friend, inside our circle of stones on the beach with the shores burning on one side of us and that dark, unknown ocean on the other side of us.

We need you to bring it—and to use your key.

And just so we're clear, by "bring" I mean embody, by "it" I mean your leadership, and by "key" I mean the feminine.

We need you to embody who you are as the feminine face of leadership—as if your life depends on it. Because I'm quite certain ours do.

You've got something for us in you, and I, for one, am damn eager for you to spit it out sooner rather than later.

Hope. Love. A new model of working. A new paradigm of education. Joy. Art. A revolutionary approach to agriculture. An innovative medical practice. Community action. A game-changing way of thinking about world religions. A powerful political platform.

Who knows? Maybe more than one—or all of them.

It doesn't matter.

What does matter is that we get all hands on this deck—including yours—working together, each showing up with something we've said yes to that is bigger than ourselves.

Plenty will opt out of this ask, and that is their privilege at work.

You get to decide if you want to show up to what is inside you—that is yours, and yours alone, to own. Or not.

But I'm hoping like crazy you'll say yes sooner than later, woman.

Because we're hungry for what only you can bring.

I love you no matter what, woman.
To the moon and back. That is very far.

Lael

• • •

Gratitude

I had so many flying buttressing and fierce gargoyles holding up the cathedral of me while writing this book that I was often tempted to yell over to Quasimodo in the bell tower and say, "Check THIS out!"

So many of you to thank, but I'll begin where I began — literally — with my mom, the first woman I ever met on this big, beautiful, blue-green planet of ours. Someone who somehow found a way to tap into her magic as a mother and believe in me, even when no one believed in her. A woman who, when I would ask, "What are you most proud of in your life?" would stand up a bit taller and say with all the love in her fierce heart: *My two daughters.* Her faith in me and what I was here to do gave me a portal through which to be born and a solid patch of earth from which to launch. Thank you, Mom. I love you.

At this point, I will stand a little taller and turn my own fierce mother's heart to look at my two boys — beautiful creatures who will always remain the source of my greatest pride, a fountain of continual joy, and the unexpected inspiration to stick the landing of this book. They might not fully appreciate this yet, but they have much of what I've written about coursing naturally through their veins as men, and I am doing what I can to make space for their gifts to flow more freely and unapologetically into the world. Thank you, Couper and Graecen. I love you.

Far beyond a flying buttress and fiercer than any gargoyle is my beloved, Todd. He is the very foundation I rested upon for emotional and spiritual nourishment as I wrote this book. He also was the director of facilities for this cathedral, patching holes in my roof when the tears tried to bring down the house, stoking the fires at the altar when it got cold and damp, and who could always

340

be heard whistling as he worked, so I knew I wasn't alone in my big cathedral that felt so very empty at times. He is my partner, my calm in the storm, and my witness in life, and I will always be grateful to him that he held my hand that day by the lake and didn't let it go. Thank you, Todd. I love you.

The women of SheChanges have so generously and courageously shared their stories with me over the years. Thank you for trusting me with them and allowing me to be your witness and to ride shotgun with you in this thing we call life. It has been the greatest honor and the gift of a lifetime that keeps on giving. My deepest gratitude to the many of you who responded immediately to my late-night texts when I asked, "Do I have your permission to use this?" with an enthusiastic *"Are you kidding? Of course, you can! I'm so honored… you have my blessing."* Little did you know that with a few quick keystrokes, I could credit that story with another woman you've probably never met—but it was you I held in my heart. Thank you, women of SheChanges. I love you.

There have been nearly seventy women who have taken the stage with me at my annual storytelling event, SheSpeaks, over the years, and I am honored and grateful to have gotten the chance to share a stage with each and every one of them. Their words and energy helped buoy me on these pages as I sought to get naked with the truth of my own story as a leader, as did the devoted and enthusiastic fans who fill the audience year after year in our beautiful town of Portland, Maine. Thank you, SheSpeaks people. I love you.

Thank you to all the women out there who have been called "lucky," "fearless," or "blessed" just one too many times. I feel you out there, and I feel your pain—and sadly your shame at times. Thank you for making your bold moves in the face of not being fully seen or understood…and thank you for not dismissing the results you yielded as an accident or a fluke. Thank you for keeping your fire lit, so we might all touch our matches to it someday when we finally see you as you *actually* are—a blessedly human woman—and not as the convenient picture we've painted of you that keeps you separate from us.

Thank you to all the women who have been "Yeah, butted" by others and told why it was "so easy" for them. I know it wasn't because I have seen behind the veil of those stories we tell ourselves. Thank you for continuing to show up as your full selves, without apology, explanation, justification, or defense at the ready. Thank you for trusting yourself to be a reliable narrator of your own life, even in the face of being written off, discounted, or summarily dismissed. Thank you for standing in the bright light of your fire and inspiring others with your bold actions so that more of us will assume responsibility for our own.

Thank you to the women who dared to believe they could be profoundly grateful and deeply hungry at the same time. Thank you for your audacity of wanting more, your moxie for breaking rank with "the way it is," your pluck for calling bullshit on your excuses and self-limiting beliefs, and showing us all how it looks.

Thank you to my kickass team of *Batch Catchers*: Jessica Esch, Susan Fekety, Noel Gallagher, Erica Labb, Elizabeth MacLaren, and Steve McCarthy. Did you think I forgot about you? Thank you for holding space—individually and collectively—so I could start listening to what was trying to come through me. Feeling your catcher's mitts at the ready every Friday afternoon for those two months gave me the courage—and the accountability—to do more than just talk about this book.

Thank you, Katie and Chris Bouton, for your gift of *The Waterhouse* to use on those lonely, long days as I was first hatching this book. This was the place in which I wrote my first book, and tapping back into that good mojo there was so critical in helping me to finally appreciate that I am truly a writer—not simply someone who stumbled on that first book by accident.

Thank you to Sue Ellen and John Simon for their annual gift of *Sundance* down in the Outer Banks. Having this place to come home to in the middle of the ocean every March has been a beacon for me like Old Baldy herself—bringing me back to myself and offering me a familiar place to roost that is surrounded by water, like my own personal Avalon.

Thank you to my dear neighbors, Kristin Chase Duffy and Jeannette Wycoff, for always being willing to meet me in the street, listen to me read aloud patches of writing, and talk through what's tightly knotted in my creative brain. The enthusiasm, witnessing, loving looks, and raucous laughter you've offered over my time on this street—especially the past two years—have greased the skids of this book and helped it to further slip out of drydock each time I came home from a writing retreat.

Thank you to my sister, Fuller Watts Crowley, for whispering to me all those years ago on the carpet of our upstairs hallway: "Just write what you want to say, Lael." And for reading everything I've written since and letting me know that what I say matters.

Thank you to my lifeline friends—a list of whom I literally keep in my phone with *call these people when you need help*—who answered my calls and loved up on me when I needed it most: Jeanne Handy, Mish Sommers, Elizabeth MacLaren, Noel Gallagher, Adele Jacques, Molly Simmons, and Sue Ellen Simon. Thank you for seeing me as more than the work I do within the context of SheChanges, and for holding space when I've needed a good laugh or a good cry in those very human moments.

Thank you to all of the badass backers of my GoFundMe campaign: Grace Brescia, Joan Fortin, Sue Ellen Simon, Lisa Whited, Katie Bouton, Anne Morin, Katie Delorme, Maddy Vertenten, Cholla Foote, Heather Parker, Nicole Provonsil, Cate Gaynor, Kelly Seiler, Sara Rivard, Robin Hodgskin, Maddie Simpson, Lisa Portelli, Amanda Downing, Nicki Fenderson, Ashley Dobbs, and Hillary

Roy. Because of you and your generous financial support, I knew beyond a doubt that this book was worth investing in. Your gifts helped me make it happen, and each time one came in, it made me feel like I was getting a divine wink from the Universe.

Thank you to Kate Northrup for always being a text away. Your voice has been the one I've reached for when I was most shaky because you know intimately what it feels like to bring a book into the world — twice. Your perfectly timed voice memos from afar and loving eyes over bowls of hot soup helped to soothe my weary soul when I needed it most.

Thank you to Susan Fekety and Noel Gallagher for your early readings of this manuscript and your gentle — yet fierce — questioning and urgings. Thank you for calling bullshit on the many ways I was hiding behind myself and for pointing to my own fire and insistently saying, *"Light it, Lael. It's time."*

Thank you to Elizabeth Holstrom and the entire DisruptHR team for calling me up — and consequently calling me out — to talk about why women are leaving organizations. Those two weeks I prepared for that five-minute story radically altered the course of this book, and I will forever be grateful for that event as the catalyst that fully — and finally — ignited the fire in me.

Thanks to the Jacques family for their generous gifting of their cottage on the rocky coast of Maine. Magic lives in that place, and the words up there flowed out of me like golden honey at a time when I needed it most. I will forever be grateful for my stays there, especially as it was being gutted and renovated, because it provided the perfect backdrop for what I was doing with my book as I revised it time and time again.

Thank you to my badass team of creatives who worked their magic to have this book come to light in all its glory. Lauryn Sophia, you were the perfect Jeep-driving kindred spirit to meet me in a muddy field to see what magic photographs would find us. Thank you for encouraging me to lean into the magic and for inviting me to get wild. Who else would trust in that craziness of making a cover before the manuscript was finalized? Nicki Fenderson of Sugarjets Studio, that's who, with her mad-skilled unicorn ways of designing something that's *exactly* what I wanted but couldn't think to imagine. The cover design you made perfectly captures what I had been conjuring in my mind's eye for years, and the typesetting inside the book still makes me swoon.

Thank you, Maddy and Joe Vertenten, who graciously offered up their beautiful farmhouse, barn, and firepit for the photoshoot for the cover of this book and then showed me all the most magical trails in the woods and views of the wild ocean nearby. It says so much about you and your love of powerful women that you didn't bat an eye when I mentioned that upwards of twenty-five women or so might be joining me at twilight…

Thank you to the fabulous, devoted, fiercely game and thoroughly enthusiastic women who made time in their busy schedules at the height of the summer season to join me in a field with little to no explanation, expectations, or directions. I loved hearing each and every one of you rally, and I will never forget the growling, roaring, and dancing by the fire that ensued. Thank you for standing behind me as I worked my magic with this: Jenn Black, Gemma Dreher, Kristin Chase Duffy, Kathryn Duffy, Pam Erickson, Susan Fekety, Cholla Foote, Joan Fortin, Josephina Gasca, Megan Hellstedt, Robin Hodgskin, Julie Hoffheimer, Adele Jacques, Tara Jenkins, Kate Knox, Corinne Mockler, Deborah Mohr, Anne Morin, Christina Neuner, Molly Neuner, Sherri Parks, and Lisa Whited.

Thank you to my editor, Nikki Van De Car at knliterary, for your deft and fierce skills that helped me to see the most luminous bits of a very large manuscript. I felt so heard and seen by you and so held in your capable hands. Thank you for helping me unleash my magic by working your own. I will forever be grateful for being called out as a witch who was hiding my full wattage.

Thank you to my copy editor, Julia Nickles, who flew into my life at just the perfect moment and made it all feel super easy and manageable. I never knew it could be like this. Your steady and calm presence in the midst of my noisy thrashing was so deeply appreciated — as was your wizardry around tenses, artful suggestions, and keen attention to detail.

Thank you to my late-night "Cover Queens" Kat Joyce, Joan Fortin, Lisa Whited, Anne Morin, Gemma Dreher, Kate Northrup, Nicole Bono, and Joanna Horton McPherson. The ability to bounce off of others is a critical part of my creative process, and you women were flying steadily with me in a V-formation right up until the end with your late-night texts and calls, helping me to see and feel my way more confidently.

Thank you to the traveling companion women I've had on this journey: Meggan Watterson, Layla Saad, Sharon Blackie, Rupi Kaur, Lisa Lister, Brené Brown, Samin Nosrat, Glennon Doye, Maya Angelou, Marie Forleo Kristi Meisenbach Boylan, Rebecca Traister, Clarissa Pinkola Estes, Elizabeth Gilbert, Barbara Kingsolver, and Tererai Trent. Your bold, provocative, and trail-blazing works have helped to keep me rooted and on my path.

And finally, a deep bow of gratitude to the fierce and divine feminine, that one who has been patiently waiting and rising up in us, again and again, like sap from our roots deep in the earth. Thank you for your tenacity and faith that we would someday reach for you. And thank you to my spiritual wing women, Mary Magdalene, Sarah-la-Kali, Lilith, Kali, and Freyja, for your steadfast and fiercely loving company — for reminding me what mattered most and giving me a strong shoulder to cry on during those dark nights of my soul.

Here's to us, fine people. And thank you.

Made in the USA
Lexington, KY
19 November 2019